Nigeria

Other Books of Related Interest:

Opposing Viewpoints Series

Canada

China

Iran

Israel

At Issue Series

Does the U.S. Two-Party System Still Work?

The Energy Crisis

Current Controversies Series

Oil

The World Economy

"Congress shall make no law . . . abridging the freedom of speech, or of the press."

First Amendment to the US Constitution

The basic foundation of our democracy is the First Amendment guarantee of freedom of expression. The Opposing Viewpoints series is dedicated to the concept of this basic freedom and the idea that it is more important to practice it than to enshrine it.

Nigeria

Margaret Haerens, Book Editor

GREENHAVEN PRESS
A part of Gale, Cengage Learning

GALE
CENGAGE Learning·

Detroit • New York • San Francisco • New Haven, Conn • Waterville, Maine • London

Elizabeth Des Chenes, *Managing Editor*

© 2012 Greenhaven Press, a part of Gale, Cengage Learning.

Gale and Greenhaven Press are registered trademarks used herein under license.

For more information, contact:
Greenhaven Press
27500 Drake Rd.
Farmington Hills, MI 48331-3535
Or you can visit our Internet site at gale.cengage.com

For product information and technology assistance, contact us at

Gale Customer Support, 1-800-877-4253
For permission to use material from this text or product, submit all requests online at www.cengage.com/permissions

Further permissions questions can be emailed to permissionrequest@cengage.com

Articles in Greenhaven Press anthologies are often edited for length to meet page requirements. In addition, original titles of these works are changed to clearly present the main thesis and to explicitly indicate the author's opinion. Every effort is made to ensure that Greenhaven Press accurately reflects the original intent of the authors. Every effort has been made to trace the owners of copyrighted material.

Cover Image © Ivan Kuzmin/Shutterstock.com.

LIBRARY OF CONGRESS CATALOGING-IN-PUBLICATION DATA

Nigeria / Margaret Haerens, book editor.
   p. cm. -- (Opposing viewpoints)
   Includes bibliographical references and index.
   ISBN 978-0-7377-5749-1 (hardcover) -- ISBN 978-0-7377-5750-7 (pbk.)
   1. Nigeria--Politics and government--21st century. 2. Nigeria--Social conditions--21st century. 3. Nigeria--Economic conditions--21st century. I. Haerens, Margaret. II. Series: Opposing viewpoints series (Unnumbered)
   JQ3090.N46 2012
   966.9--dc23
                                                              2011034330

Printed in the United States of America
1 2 3 4 5 6 7 16 15 14 13 12

Contents

Chapter 3: How Serious Is the Corruption Problem in Nigeria?

Chapter 4: What Challenges Does Nigeria Face?

Why Consider Opposing Viewpoints?

> *"The only way in which a human being can make some approach to knowing the whole of a subject is by hearing what can be said about it by persons of every variety of opinion and studying all modes in which it can be looked at by every character of mind. No wise man ever acquired his wisdom in any mode but this."*
>
> *John Stuart Mill*

In our media-intensive culture it is not difficult to find differing opinions. Thousands of newspapers and magazines and dozens of radio and television talk shows resound with differing points of view. The difficulty lies in deciding which opinion to agree with and which "experts" seem the most credible. The more inundated we become with differing opinions and claims, the more essential it is to hone critical reading and thinking skills to evaluate these ideas. Opposing Viewpoints books address this problem directly by presenting stimulating debates that can be used to enhance and teach these skills. The varied opinions contained in each book examine many different aspects of a single issue. While examining these conveniently edited opposing views, readers can develop critical thinking skills such as the ability to compare and contrast authors' credibility, facts, argumentation styles, use of persuasive techniques, and other stylistic tools. In short, the Opposing Viewpoints Series is an ideal way to attain the higher-level thinking and reading skills so essential in a culture of diverse and contradictory opinions.

In addition to providing a tool for critical thinking, Opposing Viewpoints books challenge readers to question their own strongly held opinions and assumptions. Most people form their opinions on the basis of upbringing, peer pressure, and personal, cultural, or professional bias. By reading carefully balanced opposing views, readers must directly confront new ideas as well as the opinions of those with whom they disagree. This is not to simplistically argue that everyone who reads opposing views will—or should—change his or her opinion. Instead, the series enhances readers' understanding of their own views by encouraging confrontation with opposing ideas. Careful examination of others' views can lead to the readers' understanding of the logical inconsistencies in their own opinions, perspective on why they hold an opinion, and the consideration of the possibility that their opinion requires further evaluation.

Evaluating Other Opinions

To ensure that this type of examination occurs, Opposing Viewpoints books present all types of opinions. Prominent spokespeople on different sides of each issue as well as well-known professionals from many disciplines challenge the reader. An additional goal of the series is to provide a forum for other, less known, or even unpopular viewpoints. The opinion of an ordinary person who has had to make the decision to cut off life support from a terminally ill relative, for example, may be just as valuable and provide just as much insight as a medical ethicist's professional opinion. The editors have two additional purposes in including these less known views. One, the editors encourage readers to respect others' opinions—even when not enhanced by professional credibility. It is only by reading or listening to and objectively evaluating others' ideas that one can determine whether they are worthy of consideration. Two, the inclusion of such viewpoints encourages the important critical thinking skill of objectively evaluating an author's credentials and bias. This evaluation will illuminate an author's reasons for taking a particular stance on an issue and will aid in readers' evaluation of the author's ideas.

It is our hope that these books will give readers a deeper understanding of the issues debated and an appreciation of the complexity of even seemingly simple issues when good and honest people disagree. This awareness is particularly important in a democratic society such as ours in which people enter into public debate to determine the common good. Those with whom one disagrees should not be regarded as enemies but rather as people whose views deserve careful examination and may shed light on one's own.

Thomas Jefferson once said that "difference of opinion leads to inquiry, and inquiry to truth." Jefferson, a broadly educated man, argued that "if a nation expects to be ignorant and free . . . it expects what never was and never will be." As individuals and as a nation, it is imperative that we consider the opinions of others and examine them with skill and discernment. The Opposing Viewpoints series is intended to help readers achieve this goal.

David L. Bender and Bruno Leone,
Founders

Introduction

> *"I am mindful that I represent the shared aspiration of all our people to forge a united Nigeria: a land of justice, opportunity, and plenty. Confident that a people that are truly committed to a noble ideal cannot be denied the realization of their vision, I assure you that this dream of Nigeria, that is so deeply felt by millions, will indeed come to reality."*
>
> *—Nigerian president*
> *Goodluck Jonathan,*
> *in his inauguration speech,*
> *May 29, 2011*

On May 29, 2011, Goodluck Jonathan was inaugurated as president of Nigeria. In his speech, he appealed to the people of Nigeria to help him transform the country into a thriving, peaceful, and productive nation that works to protect the rights of all its people. "We must grow the economy, create jobs, and generate enduring happiness for our people," he stated. "I have great confidence in the ability of Nigerians to transform this country. The urgent task of my administration is to provide a suitable environment, for productive activities to flourish. I therefore call on the good people of Nigeria, to enlist as agents of this great transformation." Although to some this may seem standard political rhetoric from a new president, to many Nigerians it inspires hope that the Jonathan administration will be the leadership they need to move the country forward. For them, Jonathan may be a transformative candidate who has a great opportunity to address endemic and deeply rooted problems that have hindered economic, political, and social development and have held Nigeria back from its true potential in Africa and the world.

Nigeria's problems mirror those of other African countries—and in fact, are universal. Tension between the largely Muslim north and the Christian-dominated south has frequently blown up into full-scale conflict. British colonialism left a legacy of corruption, mismanagement, and incompetence in many government bureaucracies. As a result of greed and poor government, infrastructure is old and crumbling and new projects are delayed by corruption and thievery. The Nigerian power supply is inadequate and cannot support the country's industrial ambitions—it can't even keep hospitals and existing businesses running, forcing the widespread use of pollution-spewing generators. The Niger Delta region, rich with oil and gas, has been exploited by international oil companies that have oppressed citizens in the area and have failed to provide jobs and revenue for the region. Environmental disasters go virtually unpunished and threaten the health and livelihoods of people.

Like every other country, Nigeria has a long list of serious and complex challenges. Unfortunately, one of the nation's top challenges has been competent and ethical leadership. For many years, Nigerians have been ruled by leaders who have been dogged by corruption problems. For example, Yakubu Gowon, the head of the military government that ran Nigeria for part of the 1960s and 1970s, let his corrupt governors run their states without interference, which resulted in widespread fraud, malfeasance, misuse of power, and illegal activities. The troubled administration of Shehu Shagari was accused of economic malfeasance, electoral fraud, graft, and corruption. General Ibrahim Badamasi Babangida's military government, which ruled from 1985 to 1993, is thought to have presided over one of the most corrupt administrations in the country's post-colonial era. It stands accused of election rigging, political interference, the assassination of journalists and political enemies, graft, and a number of human rights abuses. After the death of General Sani Abacha, who ruled Nigeria from 1993–1998, authorities found that billions of dollars had been siphoned from the country's accounts by him and members of his family. He also jailed and executed dissenters and political enemies, controlled the press, banned political activity, and stifled free speech.

These past leadership failures have deeply affected Nigeria's present and future. Deeply corrupt leaders like Abacha and Babangida succeeded in enriching themselves, their families, and political allies, as well as international corporations willing to reward their administrations. Tragically, to a great extent, they failed the Nigerian people. Observers note that Nigeria remained an economically stratified country without many opportunities for those not willing to indulge in the corrupt and unethical practices endemic in the political and economic system. Corrupt leaders provided poor role models for young Nigerians, who saw the way to get ahead was to cheat, lie, and steal. The Nigerians who were fighting for fairness and opportunity and justice were often jailed or harassed.

In recent years, the voices for reform in Nigeria are stronger and more confident. As Nigeria strives to become a bigger leader in Africa and the world, many observers argue that it must address its leadership problem. With the election of ethical and effective leaders, it is thought that Nigeria can confront its tolerance of corruption as well as the other problems that have hindered its progress on the world stage.

The 2011 election represented a new opportunity for Nigeria to find a leader who can do those things. In his inaugural speech, Goodluck Jonathan marked his intention to be such a leader. "My fellow countrymen and women, Nigeria is not just a land of promise; it shall be a nation where positive change will continue to take place, for the good of our people," he said. "The time for lamentation is over. This is the era of transformation. This is the time for action. But Nigeria can only be transformed if we all play our parts with commitment and sincerity. Cynicism and scepticism will not help our journey to greatness. Let us all believe in a new Nigeria. Let us work together to build a great country that we will all be proud of. This is our hour."

The authors of the viewpoints presented in *Opposing Viewpoints: Nigeria* explore the role and effectiveness of Nigeria's leadership as well as other challenges the country faces in the following chapters: Is Nigeria's Leadership Effective?, How Should Nigeria Address Violent Conflicts?, How Serious Is the Corruption Problem in Nigeria?, and What Challenges Does Nigeria Face? The information in this volume provides insight on Nigeria's domestic and foreign affairs and the issues it faces as it moves forward to cement its important place in Africa and the world.

Is Nigeria's Leadership Effective?

Chapter Preface

On April 16, 2011, Nigerians went to the polls to vote in a highly anticipated and controversial presidential election. For a country familiar with sectarian and gang violence, as well as rioting and political unrest, it would not be a stretch to predict some level of conflict between political factions. In the past, electoral cycles have featured political assassinations, voter intimidation, intra- and interparty clashes, and widespread rioting. Many observers worried that history would repeat itself. Such conflict could engulf the country quickly and threaten the fragile peace that had been painstakingly brokered between Muslims in the north and Christians in the south. Some even worried that election-day violence could spark a civil war that could break the country apart.

Since 1999 Nigeria has been electing leaders according to a power-sharing agreement, known as "zoning," which rotates political power between the largely Christian south and the largely Muslim north in the party that wins the most votes. It was hoped that the zoning agreement would prevent hostilities between Muslim and Christian factions and establish ruling equity, in which no region, religion, or ethnicity could create a monopoly of power. According to the zoning agreement, presidential power would rotate every two terms (one term is four years long) between the north and south.

In 1999, the year Nigeria returned to democracy from a long period of military dictatorship, a southern candidate, Olusegun Obasanjo, was elected. He served two terms. In 2007 a candidate from the north, Umaru Musa Yar'Adua, was elected in an election marred by charges of vote fixing, voter intimidation, and fraud. In an attempt to facilitate an era of national unity—a goal that he emphasized in his short presidency—he picked an up-and-coming politician from the south, Goodluck Jonathan, as his vice presidential candidate.

In November 2009, however, Yar'Adua left Nigeria to receive medical treatment in Saudi Arabia for pericarditis, an inflammation in the sac surrounding his heart. He was never seen in public again. His absence created a dangerous power vacuum; to address it, the Nigerian Senate transferred power to Vice President Goodluck Jonathan, who was designated as acting president until Yar'Adua had regained his health. In February 2010 Yar'Adua returned to Nigeria, but his health condition remained grim. He died on May 5, 2010.

As Nigeria mourned the loss of its president and planned a special presidential election to choose a new leader in 2011, a debate began to rage about Goodluck Jonathan's expected candidacy. Should Jonathan, a southern Christian, be eligible to run? Should the election be treated as the second term of a northern presidency, in which case only northern Muslim candidates should be eligible; or should it be considered the southern turn in the power rotation?

Goodluck Jonathan announced his candidacy for president on September 16, 2010. Also running were popular northern Muslim candidates. The debate over the zoning agreement continued to rage, and observers worried that it would boil over into serious unrest. Fortunately for the people of Nigeria, very little violence or intimidation was reported on the day of the election. On April 19, 2011, it was announced that Goodluck Jonathan was elected by 59 percent of the vote.

The concerns about the 2011 elections are explored in viewpoints included in the following chapter, which takes a look at the efficacy of Nigeria's leadership. Other viewpoints in the chapter examine Nigeria's approach to the economy, its ability to move forward and fulfill its potential, and the possibility of true and lasting reform in the nation.

"Regardless of who ultimately wins, disputed 2011 elections accompanied by increased ethnic and religious conflict would likely result in Nigeria's self-isolation from regional and continental issues."

Nigerian Elections Are Pushing the Country to the Brink of Disaster

John Campbell

John Campbell is a former US ambassador to Nigeria, the senior fellow for Africa Policy Studies at the Council on Foreign Relations, and the author of Nigeria: Dancing on the Brink. *In the following viewpoint, he speculates that the uncertainty surrounding the 2011 Nigerian presidential elections holds the potential to spark severe regional and political violence. In turn, such unrest would have risks to US national security interests by increasing Islamic radicalization among the Nigerian Muslim population. A stable and democratic Africa, he argues, is key to*

John Campbell, "Electoral Violence in Nigeria," The Council on Foreign Relations. September 2010, pp 1–6. Copyright © 2010 by The Council on Foreign Relations. All rights reserved. Reproduced by permission.

African, American, and global security interests. Campbell concludes that the United States must remain vigilant to such unrest and take steps to mitigate it if necessary.

As you read, consider the following questions:

1. According to the author, how many deaths have been attributed to ethnic, religious, and regional conflict in Nigeria since 1999?

2. How many people were killed in the violence after the contested 2008 local elections in Jos?

3. How many internally displaced people are there in Nigeria, according to Campbell?

Introduction

Nigeria is a country of overlapping regional, religious, and ethnic divisions. Rifts between the North and the South of the country, ethnic groups, and Islam and Christianity often coincide and have sometimes resulted in sectarian violence. This has been the case particularly in its geographical center and in the Niger Delta region. In the Middle Belt, as the former is called, bouts of retributive bloodshed between Christian farmers and Muslim pastoralists erupt with some frequency. In the Niger Delta, an insurrection against the Abuja government has been raging for more than a decade over regional, ethnic, and environmental grievances. In all, credible observers ascribe over twelve thousand deaths since 1999 to ethnic, religious, and regional conflict in Nigeria.

Since the end of military rule eleven years ago, Nigeria's elites have largely cordoned off national presidential elections from sectarian divisions by predetermining presidential and vice presidential victors. Their People's Democratic Party (PDP) nominates one southern Christian and one northern Muslim for the presidency and vice presidency and rigs these candidates into office. Every eight years the party rotates the office for which it nominates Christian and Muslim candidates. Excluded as it is from this process of political horse trading, known as zoning, Nigeria's ethnically and religiously fractured public has become increasingly indifferent to the country's national electoral politics.

Muslim president Umaru Yar'Adua's death in May 2010 may, however, have ended the stabilizing (if undemocratic) practice of zoning. Christian vice president Goodluck Jonathan's promotion to Nigeria's highest office in the wake of Yar'Adua's illness and death has created an opportunity for the South to retain the presidency during elections scheduled for January 2011, even though under zoning a northern Muslim should be president for the next four years. With the considerable resources available to him as an incumbent president and his Ijaw constituents in the Delta region pressuring him to stay in office, Jonathan has the means and the motive to seek a full term as president. If he chooses this course, powerful northern politicians may abandon the PDP's elite consensus and challenge his candidacy. The stage would be set for a divisive and potentially violent electoral season featuring unprecedented public involvement.

If events in Nigeria so transpire, the risks to U.S. national security interests are substantial. An Abuja government paralyzed by post-election sectarian violence or a resultant military coup would be unable to collaborate with the Obama administration in regional and continental politics at a time when conflicts in Sudan, the Democratic Republic of the Congo (DRC), and Somalia are escalating. Increased conflict would also likely reduce the flow of Nigerian oil to the international oil markets. Further, sectarian violence may spiral into a humanitarian disaster requiring an international response. While the United States has limited levers by which to steer the country clear of an electoral crisis, its special relationship with the Nigerian political class does afford it a few preventive and mitigating options.

The Contingency

The ruling People's Democratic Party is the forum in which most of Nigeria's political horse trading is done. The PDP, however, is fragile. The party has little internal discipline, no political platform or principles, and it generates little popular enthusiasm. When former president Olusegun Obasanjo ran roughshod over party rules in late 2006 to ensure that the party nominated his handpicked choices for president and vice president (Umaru Yar'Adua and Goodluck Jonathan, respectively), there was only minimal protest from party members. However, with Obasanjo no longer dominating the party, and Jonathan's potential candidacy in 2011 upsetting the regional power-sharing cycle, the possibility now exists that no stabilizing elite consensus will emerge from within the PDP.

In this context, there are three likely outcomes to the PDP nomination process that will precede the 2011 elections: (1) northern and southern elites reach an agreement to support Jonathan's candidacy; (2) Jonathan steps aside in favor of a consensus candidate from the North; or (3) no consensus candidate emerges and the PDP fragments. While each of these scenarios poses problems for Nigerian peace and stability, a divided PDP presents the highest likelihood of destabilizing post-electoral sectarian violence and a subsequent coup.

At present, Jonathan's base of support is strong. Southern elites are backing him, as are, for now, some northern governors from states with large Christian minorities. However, northern power brokers are leaning neither toward supporting Jonathan in the election nor toward rallying behind a single candidate of their own. Instead, a number of senior Muslim political figures are preparing to run their own campaigns. Former military dictators Ibrahim Babangida and Muhammadu Buhari as well as current national security adviser Aliyu

Mohammed Gusau are all poised to employ their powerful patronage networks and military connections to challenge Jonathan and each other for the presidency.

If politics continue along this trajectory, Nigeria will for the first time experience a genuine political contest in 2011 with one or more northern Muslim candidates running against Jonathan and his southern and Christian supporters. With the country's political elites divided, candidates may be tempted to use ethnic and religious identities to form local coalitions, mobilize their supporters, and smear their opponents. This process is already under way at the local and state levels in Plateau state where politicians are using their common Christian identity to build multiethnic coalitions against the Muslim Hausa-Fulani.

This dangerous political dynamic may mark the beginning of a wider pattern, in which case 2011 elections will not be a predetermined elite game characterized by popular indifference. Voters mobilized by appeals to their ethnic and religious identities will instead feel they have a real stake in the outcome and will not acquiesce to rigging as they did in 1999, 2003, and 2007. Supporters of candidates illegitimately denied the presidency would thus be more inclined to protest election irregularities violently, as happened following some of the 2007 gubernatorial elections or the 2008 Jos local elections, which left seven hundred dead. Even in the unlikely event that the elections are broadly credible, some losing candidates will almost certainly have sufficient grounds to convince their supporters that victory has been stolen, especially if the winner has a different ethnic or religious identity.

If incidents in Jos provide any indication of how electoral violence might unfold in 2011, popular rage is likely to result in attacks on police stations. And if the police are unable to suppress such violence, as was the case during the Boko Haram massacre in 2009 that left eight hundred dead, the military, which traditionally regards itself as the guarantor of the state, will be poised to step in to restore order. Either junior or senior officers could take the lead. If junior officers move first, they will likely try to remove their military superiors, as Jerry Rawlings did in Ghana in 1979 when he executed eight senior officers before assuming the presidency. Senior military officials who perceive this as an imminent possibility may take preemptive action and initiate a coup of their own. A third and equally destructive way civilian authority in Nigeria might topple is if the armed forces internally splinter along religious or regional lines, as may already be happening in Plateau state. In this scenario, rival factions may launch coups and counter-coups in a manner reminiscent of events in 1966, when a southern-led coup was followed by one led by the northern Muslim Hausa-Fulani that then set the stage for the Biafra War.

Warning Indicators of Electoral Violence

If there is no consensus PDP candidate, and elites from the Christian South and Muslim North compete openly for the Nigerian presidency, there will be two indicators that post-electoral violence might accelerate beyond Abuja's ability to suppress it: the division of the electorate into mutually hostile blocks defined by regional, ethnic, and religious identities; and inadequate preparation by the Independent National Electoral Commission (INEC) to ensure free, fair, and credible elections. Military intervention becomes more likely if elections lacking credibility are accompanied by sectarian violence. Under these circumstances, senior officers or disaffected junior officers might try to seize power.

Campaign rhetoric resorts to ethnic and religious themes. In the past, measures outlawing confessional or regionally based political parties largely kept ethnicity and religion out of elections. However, an open field of candidates no longer restrained by power-sharing raises the possibility that some candidates will rally support by appealing to ethnic and religious

Power Sharing, or "Zoning," in Nigeria

Given the ethnic and religious complexities of Nigeria— and the recurring cycles of violence between communities of the north and south since independence—the ruling PDP [People's Democratic Party] adopted "zoning" or power rotation in the interests of what it called equity. According to this idea, power should be rotated between the largely Christian south and the largely Muslim north.

Goodluck Jonathan—who as a southern Christian was chosen as [Umaru] Yar'Adua's running mate under the same equity principle—took over as president after months of confusion and debate. Was he acting president or would he enjoy substantive powers? For their part, Jonathan's constituency, the minorities of the restive Niger Delta, insist that Jonathan should now contest the next election, saying the north's term in office—while brief—is now over.

Underlying all this, of course, is the assumption that the PDP will remain unchallenged at the polls. Up until the elections of 2007, which by common consent of election observers was the worst election ever held in Nigeria, this could be guaranteed. But things have changed. President Jonathan recently appointed a respected academic, Attahiru Jega, to head the Independent National Electoral Commission [INEC], and gave the INEC 87 billion naira ($580 million) to keep the next elections free and fair. Yet, since political office still means access to oil revenues, the influence of corruption is difficult to eradicate.

Adewale Maja-Pearce, "Nigeria's 2011 Presidential Race Tests North-South Powersharing Agreement," Christian Science Monitor, *August 16, 2010.*

identities. Local radio stations, particularly those that cater to the dominant ethnic group in a given area, are the primary medium through which these messages would be transmitted. Political operatives may, however, also spread rumors and defamation ads via websites and social networking tools such as Twitter and Facebook. Neither the print press nor national television networks are likely to propagate such inflammatory rhetoric. Outbreaks of violence this year in the Middle Belt offer evidence of the damage these messages can create: a series of text messages stirred up lingering resentment from the disputed elections of 2008 and resulted in the tit-for-tat massacre of fifteen hundred people.

The presidency fails to implement the new legislation passed by the National Assembly to secure the autonomy of INEC and provide the necessary funding. Up until now, the presidency has controlled and funded INEC. Without fiscal independence from the executive, an incumbent president has latitude to manipulate INEC in his favor, and Nigerians will not trust the results the commission announces. Election outcomes lacking credibility could, in turn, create substantial space for violent opposition by the losing candidate(s), especially where the contests have a sectarian cast.

INEC fails to implement a credible registration system, a credible ballot and ballot box distribution process, or a transparent ballot-counting procedure. At present, there is no credible voter role, though INEC promises one by November, and there has been little or no preparation for delivering, securing, and counting ballots. Absent these elements, the state governors and their agents will easily rig elections as former governor of Cross Rivers Donald Duke detailed in a July article in the *Guardian* of Lagos. As with transparent INEC pandering to the president, blatant corruption of this sort is very likely to induce violence in a polarized electoral environment.

Efforts to restrict military movement or overt signs of divisions within the military. While a junior officer coup would likely come without warning, signs that senior military personnel fear a coup by junior officers and may be preparing their own seizure of power include official restrictions on troop movements, as occurred in December 2009, or exhortations that soldiers remain nonpolitical. Should soldiers in uniform assert their ethnic and religious identities, which would be evident if they refuse to obey orders in a sectarian conflict, the senior military leadership is also likely to assume control of the state.

Potential Implications for the United States

If Jonathan does not emerge victorious in the 2011 elections, there will likely be greater militant activity in the Niger Delta. The militants are mostly Jonathan's fellow Ijaws, an ethnic group that sees his candidacy as providing them with a seat at the national table for the first time since independence. If thwarted by Jonathan's exclusion from power, they are likely to abandon the restraint they usually show in their attacks on the petroleum industry. It is an open secret that militants could easily shut down Nigeria's oil industry. If this occurs, the impact on the international oil market would be great: In 2008, militant-group attacks on Nigeria's oil infrastructure caused a major drop in the country's total output, which in turn helped raise oil prices to $150 per barrel. However, it is more likely that the militants would attempt to seize production facilities instead of destroying them, albeit with collateral damage resulting in a greater loss of production than the militants would have wanted. The Nigerian military—numbering less than one hundred thousand with obligations in other parts of the country—probably lacks the capacity to dislodge militants from oil production facilities once they are captured. In the past, it has not been able to overcome the militants in the Delta through military force except for certain isolated instances. It may nevertheless attempt to do so and cause bloodshed in the process.

The victory of a southern Christian in a rigged presidential election would, on the other hand, open the door to greater radicalization of northern Nigeria's Islamic population. Fragmented northern elites and traditional religious authorities are already losing stature as the impoverished population turns to nontraditional and occasionally radical religious leadership. If a southern-dominated Jonathan government further marginalizes the North in the distribution of government jobs and oil revenue, this trend may worsen. Up to now, such Islamic radicalization has been inward-looking, opposing the secular government in Abuja rather than the western "Great Satan." Nevertheless, intensified Islamic radicalization could open new space for international terrorist groups hostile to the United States. An al-Qaeda-trained Nigerian has already tried to blow up a Northwest flight over Detroit. There could be more such episodes if an alienated North becomes a hospitable environment for new, non-indigenous, radical forms of Islam.

Regardless of who ultimately wins, disputed 2011 elections accompanied by increased ethnic and religious conflict would likely result in Nigeria's self-isolation from regional and continental issues. As occurred during Yar'Adua's prolonged illness and Nigeria's concurrent weak regional leadership vis-à-vis the political crises in Guinea and Niger, the United States would lose an important diplomatic partner with respect to Darfur, southern Sudan, and the Horn of Africa. In the past, the international community has been particularly dependent on Nigeria to provide peacekeepers for United Nations missions such as those in Liberia and Darfur. With the impending referendum on succession in southern Sudan, continuing uncertainties in the Democratic Republic of the Congo, and the deteriorating situation in Somalia, Nigeria's diplomatic and military leadership again appears crucial for peace and security in Africa.

Protracted electoral violence in 2011 could also result in a humanitarian catastrophe. There are already an estimated 1.2 million internally displaced people in Nigeria, and that number would skyrocket should violence spread. The small, weak states that surround Nigeria are not, moreover, prepared to handle even small refugee flows. Media coverage of a humanitarian disaster would therefore surely prompt calls for international assistance, even if a military coup precluded any such intervention. Though its methods would be rough, a united military government would likely respond to such a humanitarian crisis by quickly restoring public order.

The return of military dictatorship to the "giant of Africa" would nonetheless severely undercut the African Union (AU) and Economic Community of West African States' (ECOWAS) principled opposition to coups and further isolate the country from the international community. The United States in particular would lose what little rhetorical leverage it has if, as in previous military takeovers, the chief of state is relatively unconcerned with his country's international profile. U.S. laws requiring sanctions and aid cuts to the new military regime would place yet more distance between Washington and Abuja. In the worst of all possible scenarios, the military itself might divide along ethnic and religious lines. Factions struggling for power could initiate a series of coups and counter-coups, and perhaps even introduce the specter of warlordism.

Disputed elections and resulting sectarian conflict or a military coup d'état would lastly undermine democracy's standing among Nigeria's neighbors and throughout Africa. Though over the long term the country might benefit from a breakup of the PDP's current monopoly that creates political space for opposition parties, over the short term, widespread post-electoral violence would put Nigeria in a class with Zimbabwe, Sudan, and Kenya as a failing state whose instability threatens its neighbors and requires prolonged international engagement.

> "I have long argued that the Nigerian nation has come into existence, over and beyond its constituent ethnic and religious parts."

Nigerian Elections Will Not Push the Country into Chaos

THISDAY

THISDAY *is one of Nigeria's daily newspapers. In the following viewpoint, the author agrees with former US ambassador John Campbell that Nigeria is in great danger of falling into unrest and violence. However, it is not because of the elections that the state of the country is so precipitous; it is because Nigeria has been laboring under one-party rule and in the grip of a powerful military dictatorship that is unable and unwilling to meet the needs of its people. Unlike Campbell, who believes religious and ethnic forces will spark sectarian conflicts that will break the country apart, THISDAY argues that the danger comes from economic frustration and that America should be focusing on Nigerian reformers who hope to bring about an era of true democratic governance.*

As you read, consider the following questions:

1. When does the author say that the ruling PDP came into power?

2. According to the viewpoint, what is the only difference between the PDP and the military dictatorship it replaced?

3. When was John Campbell the US ambassador to Nigeria?

Is Nigeria dancing on the edge of the cliff right now? The answer is an unequivocal yes. The democratic transition, resumed twelve years ago, is on a cliff-hanger as elite politicians squabble over not what direction to take an impoverished and increasingly traumatized people but who among them has the right to contest the presidency in 2011. The ruling People's Democratic Party (PDP), in power since May 1999, has proved singularly unable to order its own house. The PDP has not been able to deliver prosperity and national stability. It has not been able to deliver a sense of well-being among Nigerians. If anything, ordinary Nigerians now say that they feel worse off than ever before.

It would not have constituted much of a problem if the PDP, one of over fifty political parties in the country, were a proper party, subjecting itself to the rigour of the polls every four years. Since a small group of retired army generals and their civilian friends gathered in conclave in 1998 and chose Olusegun Obasanjo and the PDP as the instruments through which their grip on the country would continue in new 'civilian' guise, the party has grown into an African colossus. It regularly rigs itself back to power despite the widespread protests of a populace that say that the party has no answer to their pressing problems. The party has also been able to transform its grip on the country's strategic resources, including the federal treasury, into the lethal machine with which it sucks life out of rival parties, compelling otherwise decent but impoverished opposition politicians to seek shelter under its morally crippling umbrella.

Nigeria Is Not a Proper Democracy

The net result is what we have today: 'democracy' without a proper ruling political party rooted in democratic culture. It is also 'democracy' without citizenship for the simple reason that an impoverished people whose civic culture has atrophied after several decades of brutal and corrupt military dictatorship cannot be full and active citizens participating in public affairs and shaping public policy to meet their needs. It was Fareed Zakaria, the writer and journalist, who characterized 'democracies' of this sort that have been emerging in Asia, Africa, Latin America and Eastern Europe since the end of the Cold War, flaunting regular 'elections' but without the liberal culture that only strong and autonomous civic institutions can foster as 'illiberal democracy.' They are democracies only in name. When you come closer and peer through the window it is yesterday's army general, but with his swagger stick tucked away from view, that is sitting on the president's chair.

Why is it that it was Olusegun Obasanjo, a retired general that took over as soon as the armed forces quit in 1999? Why is it that the only serious challenge to Obasanjo in 2003, when he made a bid for a second term, came from Muhammadu Buhari, another retired general? Why is it that the only credible challenge within the PDP to the present incumbent is Ibrahim Babangida, yet another retired general? The answer is simple and straightforward. Nigeria is still under the grip of a powerful military dictatorship, albeit one that has had to make a small concession by asking the soldiers to retreat to the barracks while the generals remain the public face of power. The only difference between the PDP and the armed forces it replaced is that the former uses rigged elections to take power while the army prefers the barrel of the gun. But it all comes down to the same thing: unaccountable power in the service of private ends. In military dictatorships, citizens don't rule. Dictators, in military uniform or civilian garb do. This is the case with Nigeria today, as indeed it has been since 1966.

Campbell Is Right, but for the Wrong Reason

Dr John Campbell, American ambassador to Nigeria from 2004 to 2007, was therefore right when he pointed out in his essay 'Nigeria on the Brink: What Happens if the 2011 Elections Fail?' that Nigerians have been dancing on the edge of the precipice for several years but that this time there is a real possibility that they could plunge right in where previously they had managed to step back in the nick of time. Military dictatorships tend to be stable until either of two things happen: The people, after putting up with misery and misrule for so long, one fine day decide that enough is enough, or there is a falling out among the generals over how to continue to share the loot, resulting in a bloody fight for the position of top dog.

In Nigeria's case, the two are now happening at the same time. It is not merely a coincidence that one of the better organized pressure groups that played an important role in pressuring the National Assembly to cede power to Goodluck Jonathan after President Umaru Yar'Adua took ill in November 2009 and his cabinet moved to usurp power was named 'Enough Is Enough.' They were only giving voice to the Nigerian street, at last fed up with a PDP that has not given them jobs and health care and hospitals and security. Nor is it a coincidence that in the still-intense struggle between southern PDP politicians and their northern counterparts, not a single word has been uttered about policies and programmes, and how they might be fine-tuned to speak more effectively to the complaints of Nigerian citizens. The power-sharing consensus amongst the dictators, hastily cobbled together in 1998–1999 to enable Obasanjo, a southerner to take power, and renewed albeit reluctantly in 2003, has irretrievably broken down. Since there is no honour among dictators, they are now fighting dirty among themselves, and the general concern, rightly expressed by John Campbell, is that this fight could spill into the Nigerian street, taking the country to the edge and beyond.

No Religious or Ethnic Conflict

I however do not share the ambassador's thesis that religious and ethnic fault lines are likely to provide the tinder for this implosion, and that the armed forces could intervene as the ultimate guarantor of national unity. I have long argued that the Nigerian nation has come into existence, over and beyond its constituent ethnic and religious parts. The latter are still powerful social players, but are increasingly taking the back seat as ordinary Nigerians traverse the country in search of daily bread. And whenever they have been given the opportunity to vote in clean elections, the voting has always demonstrated a powerful tilt towards larger Nigerian nationhood.

Nor is there any real danger that the armed forces could come back. Nigerians may be sick of corrupt PDP politicians, but they have not forgotten what the soldiers did to them only yesterday. In any case, rigged elections amount to a coup d'état, and the PDP has repeatedly done this since 1999. Dr Campbell rightly drew attention to the fact that Nigerian democrats are asking for Nuhu Ribadu [the former head of the Economic and Financial Crimes Commission (EFCC)] and his tribe of change makers to be given an opportunity to take a shot at political power. The question is: How can the Ribadus in our country, standing for probity and change, be empowered by ordinary Nigerians who clearly want to save their country to move from a 'long shot' to real contenders for power?

This, indeed, is the direction American policy makers should be focusing their attention right now.

> *"Full participation in this coming general election will give way for a free people to govern themselves, freedom of expression and [to] enjoy good governance and accountability. This [year's] general election will provide [the] greatest avenue for [the] greatest development in Nigeria."*

Elections Are a Chance to Finally Get Things Right in Nigeria

Adewale T. Akande

Adewale T. Akande is an educator and author. In the following viewpoint, he perceives the 2011 presidential election as a prime opportunity for the Nigerian people to throw off the yoke of corruption, incompetence, and repression and usher in a new era. Akande argues that it is essential for all eligible citizens to register and vote for the best candidate—regardless of political affiliation—in order to get their voices heard and affect real and lasting change in the country. That is the only way, Akande asserts, to reclaim Nigeria's lost democracy and put in place an enduring democratic culture.

As you read, consider the following questions:

1. What does Akande believe will happen to all bad politicians as a result of the 2011 elections?

2. What does the author cite as the long-running motto of Nigeria?

3. What accomplishment does Akande view as essential to boosting national socioeconomic development and encouraging foreign investment?

Every journey starts with the first small step. There is no doubt that this year's [2011] general election will definitely change the course of history of Nigeria for a new nation. Nigerians have learnt their lessons in a very hard way. Nigerians have come to realize that they are the solution to their problems. Suffering is how we react to events that happen to us.

A New Era

Most Nigerian problems are self-created and [Nigerians] now realise that their destiny is in their hands. This coming election will reveal to all and sundry that relationship between citizens and the state is fundamental to democracy. The journey to a new Nigeria after fifty years of independence begins this year. This is the year that the catastrophes of past regimes will be turned to greatest opportunities by all eligible voters that cast their votes for a great change. I am foreseeing a decisive year in the history of this country when all Nigerians will decide to participate and usher in a government of the people by the people and for the people. This is going to be a year of true and functioning democracy where many voices expressing different or even contrary ideas and opinions will do it without fear or intimidation. This is the year Nigerians will detox their negative thoughts, forget the imbalances of the past and get themselves into a positive frame of mind that will inspire them to come out en masse and vote for a set of leaders that can re-write the history of Nigeria.

The game is up for all inept and dubious politicians. Now is the time for bad-belle, do-or-die politicians to look for another job. It is time for all political opportunists, thugs, [and] criminals to go back to the farms. Nigerians have realised that they have missed good things of life from those selfish and mischievous politicians and now [must unite] to bring back those missing beauties of democracy. This is the time to change from obscurity to reality and from disappointments to opportunities. This is the time we will all say goodbye to politics of hatred and deceit. Full participation in this coming general election will give way for a free people to govern themselves, freedom of expression and [to] enjoy good governance and accountability. This [year's] general election will provide [the] greatest avenue for [the] greatest development in Nigeria.

Imagine

Imagine a new Nigeria where its age-long motto "Unity and Faith, Peace and Unity" to have practical meanings to all Nigerians; where oneness, harmony, trust, understanding, reconciliation and development take its root in all regions. A country where there will be love, unity and peace among the Kanuris, the Fulanis, the Hausas, the Gbagyis (Gwarris), the Tivs, the Nupes, the Yorubas, the Edos, the Urhobos, the Igbos, the Ijaws and the Ibibios. Where there is no love, unity, peace and progress can never exist; where deep ethnic, regional and [religious] violence will no longer be a national issue.

Imagine a new Nigeria where the new emerging unpolluted or uncorrupted leaders with integrity and capabilities will proudly lead us to the path of functioning democracy, good governance and accountability; a leader who will be able to interpret the present situation of the country and offer credible strategies to resolve it and transform the country within [the] shortest time. By the time we have a true leader who will be ready to lay down his life for the progress of the country, then you will know that we have been unfortunate with those past leaders. New leaders, who will dedicate all their effort to leave worthy legacies and footprints on the sand of time, [will be] remembered and cherished forever. Where leaders will be servants of the people and the people will be their pay-masters. Leaders that realise that greatness is not property accumulated within [the] shortest time but the services rendered for the good of others. Since the British colonialists lowered the Union Jack and freed a land they have ruled for less than a century, the country has never enjoyed a credible leadership with good governance.

Imagine a new country where electricity and drinkable water supply will be undisrupted in twenty-four hours. This new development tonic will surely boost the national socio-economic development and encourage foreign investment in our country. This is possible in a few months with a reliable leader and government. Achieving this Guinness book of record as [the] highest buyer of electric generating machine will be removed. Imagine a new Nigeria where there is free, competitive and qualitative education for all citizens; where illiteracy and poverty levels will be reduced drastically. Imagine a nation with reliable and efficient health services without any need to travel abroad for medical checkups and treatment. A country where all local government councils will have health centres within their official site to all and sundry.

A Beautiful Thought

Imagine a new country where . . . "the police shall be employed for the prevention and detention of crime, the apprehension of offenders, the preservation of law and order, the protection of life and property and the due enforcement of all

2011 Presidential Election

PARTY	VOTES	MARGIN
PDP	22,495,187	58.89%
CPC	12,214,853	31.98%
ACN	2,067,301	5.41%
ANPP	917,012	2.40%
Others	504,866	1.32%

PDP = People's Democratic Party

CPC = Congress for Progressive Change

ACN = Action Congress of Nigeria

ANPP = All Nigeria Peoples Party

TAKEN FROM: Nigeria Elections Coalition, 2011.
http://nigeriaelections.org.

laws and regulations . . ." and not employed to collect bribes on the roads, aid criminals and dance to the tune of politicians. A new country where the "vision" of a Nigerian police force—"making the country safer and secured for the attainment of national aspiration" and the "mission" which is "to deliver qualitative and efficient security and law enforcement services to the citizens of Nigeria" will be practically implemented.

Imagine the country with the largest crude oil production and the second largest oil reserves in Africa will provide abundant fuel and gas for its citizens at very low prices. Where queuing at the petrol stations to buy fuel and kerosene will be a taboo. Where all the gains of our God-given oil and gas will be judiciously distributed to deserving regions and not to the banks of selfish and wicked so-called leaders and collaborators.

A Clarion Call

Imagine a country with modern, good and safe road and rail network services that link all the thirty-six states of federation and Abuja together. Every Nigerian has the right to travel, live and work in safety. We all have the right to walk, ride and drive on good and safe roads. A country where road safety improvement action plans [be implemented for] young and old drivers, pedestrians, motorcyclists, occupant protection, behavioural countermeasures, speed, seat belt, drunk and impaired drivers . . . in order to minimise accidents on our roads. A nation where expenditure on road safety should be used judiciously to reduce increasing numbers of Nigerians being killed daily and subsequent trauma felt by their families.

This is a clarion call for all eligible voters to come out en masse for registration exercise so that they can be able to vote during the next general election. You just have to register before you . . . vote. With the present electoral commission . . . , there is no doubt that there is power in our votes to influence the outcome of the election. Our votes this time around will give us a voice and effect the changes we have been looking [for] from a new nation. Low turnout this time can give inept and dubious politicians and their party more opportunity to cling to power. The country is fifty years old, but we are not [destined] to be living in darkness, in abject poverty, irregular water and petrol supply with our God-given human and natural resources. There is need for a change. That change will only be possible this year with our votes. We must vote for the best candidate, even if he or she does not belong to our party. We must prefer meritocracy to mediocrity. This is the only way to have leaders that can achieve good governance and accountability. Together we can reclaim our lost democracy and hope for a brighter future with free, fair, competitive and peaceful elections.

> "While it will be unfair to tar every Nigerian politician with this black brush, it is no longer in dispute that ideological prostitution is now a distinct characteristic of the nation's political culture."

There Is Little Hope That Elections Will Facilitate Real Change in Nigeria

Dafe Onojovwo

Dafe Onojovwo is a Nigerian political columnist. In the following viewpoint, he expresses his pessimism that the 2011 presidential elections will bring about any significant reform in Nigeria. Onojovwo derides Nigerian politicians as lacking political and personal integrity, willing to throw ideological principles to the wind for money or power. Voters, he contends, are easily distracted by bitter geopolitical wrangling—focusing on where the candidates come from instead of the quality of the candidate—and opposition parties do not have the resources to compete with the ruling People's Democratic Party (PDP). Overall, Onojovwo does not hold out much hope for the Nigerian people.

As you read, consider the following questions:

1. What does the author think that the Goodluck Jonathan campaign is trying to justify?

2. Why does the author think that northern candidates will have a better showing in the 2011 elections than southern candidates?

3. What does the author claim is the main issue of the campaign?

I feel no excitement as the electoral campaigns race to a climax, but only anxiety and disappointment that the country's electoral process is still entrapped by intrigue, violence, sham and confusion. In trying to understand why the political campaigns sound so hollow in their rhetoric, why brutal bloodletting is spreading from one campaign rally to another across the country, and why a sense of hope is so scarce to perceive as Election Day rapidly approaches, the basic explanation I discern is one of greed and insincerity.

Political Opportunism and Expediency

The political parties have thrown to the winds any pretence to ideological integrity. I confess my inability to distinguish between the core principles of one party and another—as manifest in actual practice. Their members, steeped in political harlotry, have, with only a few exceptions, crossed so often from party to party that their ideological sense of direction was lost long ago—traded away for expediency and opportunism. While it will be unfair to tar every Nigerian politician with this black brush, it is no longer in dispute that ideological prostitution is now a distinct characteristic of the nation's political culture. Evidence of it is everywhere as the April [2011] poll draws closer, and this is partly responsible for the sense of cynicism—and lack of excitement, or hope—with which the electorate receive the politicians' messages.

In other words, the politician here, perhaps more than elsewhere, is not trusted to stay the course or keep his word. Worsening this tendency to an unreliable character is a general lack of competence or the absence of a commitment to excellence in service. On what, therefore, is the perceptive voter to pin his faith when he listens to the ongoing campaign promises that are scarcely backed by any well-thought-out plans of implementation? It is a sobering thought to realise that after May 29 [2011], when the new government will be inaugurated based on the results of the polls, power supply is not expected to improve; and the crises in transportation, health care, water supply, education, security, the judiciary and all other facets of our national life will remain with us for a long time, tormenting and taunting the citizens.

Facing the Truth in Nigeria

I agree that this may be seen as a pessimistic view; but perhaps it is also fair to say that it is a view rooted in a realistic assessment of the situation. Why is there so much violence—so much killing, arson and vandalism—accompanying the politicians' efforts to persuade the electorate to vote for them? If commitment to serving the public and improving the people's happiness was their true motive, would a peaceful campaign be impossible? Why are candidates' names being illicitly substituted? Why is internal party strife so vicious? Why are political parties selling their platforms to any flag bearer that is the highest bidder or that is backed by the most powerful godfather? At the national level, hope is imbued or rekindled in a people when statesmen and women utilise a season of constitutional change of government, such as Nigeria is now undergoing, to articulate with passion their clear vision of the way out of the country's challenges and crises.

The 2011 Election

It has hardly been so with the 2011 campaigns. Voters have instead been distracted by bitter wrangling in the ruling party over which geopolitical zone has a right to keep power for another four or eight years, and whose turn it will be thereafter. The entire Goodluck Jonathan campaign so far has been an effort to justify the decision of a South-South indigene to exercise his constitutional right to vie for the country's highest office, when the "unexpired term" of another part of the country remains un-utilised, following the death of the last president. Every other issue has been subordinate to this question of whether the power-zoning formula of a political party is superior to the provisions of the national Constitution. In the end, it is unlikely if the performance of the Jonathan administration in office will determine the general pattern of voting in the presidential election. More crucial will be whether he manages to get the geopolitical balancing act right, through a mixture of placation and arm-twisting—carrot and stick.

The opposition candidates seem to lack the financial and logistical muscle to organise an effective grassroots campaign to dislodge the behemoth that the ruling party has become over the last 12 years in power. What hope they have to eat into the power base of the People's Democratic Party depends almost entirely on geopolitical forces, not ideological persuasiveness or personal charisma. Which will help to explain why it is northern candidates like Muhammadu Buhari (CPC [Congress for Progressive Change, a left-wing political party]), Nuhu Ribadu (ACN [Action Congress of Nigeria, a classical liberal political party]) and Ibrahim Shekarau (ANPP [All Nigeria Peoples Party, a conservative political party]) that stand a chance to make a reasonable showing in the coming presidential poll, not any southern opposition candidate, however brilliant or statesmanlike. The main issue of the campaign is still geopolitical, no matter how that fact may be disguised. It is a primordial election. That is why I'm not excited.

Periodical and Internet Sources Bibliography

The following articles have been selected to supplement the diverse views presented in this chapter.

Gab Ajuwa	"Jonathan: What Nigeria Needs for Change," *Vanguard*, March 18, 2011.
Anthony A. Kila	"The Folly of Nigerian Governors," Sahara Reporters, June 29, 2011. http://saharareporters.com.
Adewale Maja-Pearce	"Nigeria's 2011 Presidential Race Tests North-South Powersharing Agreement," *Christian Science Monitor*, August 16, 2010.
Adam Nossiter	"An Accidental Leader Stirs Hopes in Nigeria," *New York Times*, February 19, 2010.
Moses E. Ochonu	"Is Goodluck Nigeria's Bad Luck?," *Osun Defender*, March 23, 2011.
Dele Olojede	"Fair Vote, Fragile Future," *New York Times*, April 21, 2011.
Alex Perry	"Will Goodluck Jonathan Bring Good Luck to Nigeria?," *Time*, April 18, 2011.
Jeffrey D. Sachs	"Nigeria's Historic Opportunity," *New York Times*, May 30, 2011.
Leonard Karshima Shilgba	"That Nigerians May Stand Up," PointBlankNews.com, March 20, 2011. www.pointblanknews.com.
Joe Trippi	"Why Nigeria Will Not Need a 'Tahir Moment,'" *Huffington Post*, March 23, 2011. www.huffingtonpost.com.

OPPOSING
VIEWPOINTS®
SERIES

CHAPTER 2

How Should Nigeria Address Violent Conflicts?

Chapter Preface

In 2011 the small West African country of the Ivory Coast, also known by its French name Côte d'Ivoire, erupted into political conflict. What began as a contested presidential election quickly became a bloody clash between government security forces and opposition supporters. As horrible fighting engulfed the country and refugees from the conflict began to spill into other West African nations, Nigeria became one of the strongest voices in the African Union to call for military intervention to quell the violence.

The 2010 Ivorian presidential election pitted the incumbent president, Laurent Gbagbo, against the opposition leader, Alassane Ouattara. On December 2, 2010, the results were announced by the Independent Electoral Commission (IEC)—Ouattara had won the election with 54.1 percent of the vote. However, Gbagbo's government quickly announced that the results were invalid. The next day, the Constitutional Council announced that Gbagbo had won the election and sealed the country's borders. Both Gbagbo and Ouattara declared victory and took the oath of office.

The international community, including the United Nations (UN), the African Union, the European Union, and the United States, affirmed their support for Ouattara and called for Gbagbo to step down peacefully. Gbagbo refused, and ordered all UN peacekeepers to leave the country. The UN refused. Negotiation between the camps was initiated, in the hope that the situation could still be resolved without violence.

Those hopes were short-lived. In the weeks after the standoff between Gbagbo and Ouattara began, sporadic violence erupted between the two men's supporters. Gbagbo was still in control of security forces, which clashed repeatedly with Ouattara's camp. Gbagbo's supporters began attacking UN offices and businesses, and roaming the streets looking for and brutally murdering opposition members. Ouattara's supporters retaliated. Gbagbo's supporters carried out massacres of innocent civilians and then buried the bodies in mass graves. By March 2011, an estimated half a million Ivorians had fled the country in fear.

As the Ivory Coast conflict escalated, the African Union began to debate whether to intervene militarily in order to bring peace to the troubled region. The African Union brings together fifty-three African states to work together on a number of different issues, including peacekeeping activities. Another African organization, the Economic Community of West African States (ECOWAS), led by Nigerian president Goodluck Jonathan, was in favor of military intervention and formulated a plan for such an action. To launch such an ambitious effort, however, ECOWAS would have to get permission from both the African Union and the UN.

Many Nigerians favored intervention in the region, arguing that as one of the more powerful nations in West Africa, Nigeria had a responsibility to help its neighbor and prevent the situation from devolving into a full-blown civil war that would destabilize the entire region. Critics of the plan denounced interfering in the affairs of a fellow West African country and viewed intervention as a declaration of war. Others worried that with a large number of Nigerian immigrants living in the Ivory Coast any kind of military intervention would seal a death warrant for any Nigerian in the country. Some pointed out that Nigeria would be expected to provide the bulk of the forces for the ECOWAS mission, since they have the biggest and most advanced army in West Africa. These critics argued that Nigeria should be focusing on its own domestic problems—like poverty and inadequate infrastructure—instead of throwing around its weight in foreign affairs.

On April 11, 2011, Laurent Gbagbo was arrested by Ouattara's forces and French troops. Human rights organizations reported that the four-month conflict resulted in the deaths of more than a thousand people and uprooted the lives of more than a million Ivorian citizens.

For Nigeria, the conflict underscored the country's dominant role in the region and illuminated its obligation in mediating and intervening in West African conflicts. The debate over military intervention is explored in the following chapter, which covers how Nigeria should address violent conflicts. In addition to the Ivory Coast situation, viewpoints also touch on the fighting in the Niger Delta and the brutal violence in the Plateau region.

| "The massive investment the international community has made in peace and security in West Africa for nearly two decades is under threat."

Nigeria Should Be Among the Countries That Intervene in the Ivory Coast Conflict

Louise Arbour

Louise Arbour is the president of the International Crisis Group. In the following viewpoint, she expresses the concern of the International Crisis Group over the deteriorating security situation in the Ivory Coast that has exploded into a full-scale civil war over the disputed results of the November 2010 presidential election. The group recommends that the Economic Community of West African States (ECOWAS) and the African Union should intervene in order to defuse the violence and provide a political solution to the crisis. As a member of both ECOWAS and the African Union, Arbour asserts, Nigeria should be at the forefront of any military, economic, or political effort in regard to the Ivory Coast conflict.

As you read, consider the following questions:

1. Which Ivory Coast presidential candidate was confirmed by the Peace and Security Council of the African Union on March 10, 2011?

2. How many people did the United Nations report as dead because of the conflict in the Ivory Coast?

3. Who is the incumbent president of the Ivory Coast, whose refusal to accept the presidential election results sparked the conflict?

We are deeply concerned about the worsening security situation in Côte d'Ivoire [the Ivory Coast] and urge enhanced efforts to stop the country's slide into full-scale civil war, which would likely involve ethnic cleansing and other mass atrocity crimes. On 10 March 2011, the Peace and Security Council of the African Union ended the debate on the outcome of Côte d'Ivoire's 28 November 2010 presidential election by endorsing the report of the panel of the five heads of state who confirmed Alassane Ouattara as the sole legitimate president of the country. Unfortunately, this pronouncement has done little to relieve the crisis, because the incumbent regime responded with renewed armed attacks on Ouattara supporters and violent repression of the population.

The Worsening Situation in the Ivory Coast

Daily attacks on civilians, including reports of forced disappearances, rapes and torture, continue, and the death toll far exceeds the UN's confirmed count of 440 dead. Fighting between forces loyal to incumbent President Laurent Gbagbo and those allied to Alassane Ouattara has increased, including the use of heavy weapons, and widespread population displacement paralleled by hate speech and incitement to violence are worrying indicators of a deepening crisis and the potential for ethnic cleansing and other forms of mass killing. Côte d'Ivoire is no longer on the brink of civil war; it has already begun.

The Economic Community of West African States (ECOWAS [an economic alliance of fifteen West African countries]), with the support of the African Union [a union consisting of fifty-three African countries], should offer Gbagbo a final chance for a peaceful departure, while actively preparing to oust his regime by all necessary means before it is too late. The massive investment the international community has made in peace and security in West Africa for nearly two decades is under threat.

A Threat to West Africa

In a 3 March [2011] report, the International Crisis Group identified three scenarios in the short term: "decay and lasting division of the country", "social crisis and popular insurrection", and "civil war". We stressed that the civil war scenario accompanied by civilian massacres was the most likely, and that the situation in Côte d'Ivoire constituted a serious and imminent threat to peace and security throughout West Africa. Unfortunately, the facts on the ground are proving us correct.

People should not be misled by Gbagbo's appeal for inter-Ivorian dialogue and his call for an end to the violence, delivered through the spokesman for his unrecognised government on 18 March. The outgoing president did not make a clear and definitive recognition of Ouattara's election win, and the following day, Gbagbo's Minister for Youth, Charles Blé Goudé, called on young Ivorians to enlist in the army en masse "to free Côte d'Ivoire from bandits".

The future Gbagbo proposes for his country is war, anarchy and violence, with ethnic, religious and xenophobic dimensions. Ivorian state television, which is controlled by the outgoing regime, recently aired images of the bodies of rebels

killed by security forces, described as nationals of other countries in West Africa, namely Burkina Faso, Senegal and Mali,
which in the context of years of indoctrination through xenophobic rhetoric is open encouragement for reprisals against
immigrant communities.

Intervention Is Vital

ECOWAS must not give in to Gbagbo's blackmail. The physical and economic security of West African nationals living in
Côte d'Ivoire will never be secured by a regime that coarsely
manipulates the rhetoric of solidarity with "brother countries"
while threatening their citizens and unleashing militias to ter-
rorise opponents. All of West Africa faces the risk of being severely weakened by the return to civil war in Côte d'Ivoire
and the disintegration of its central government. ECOWAS
must now take decisive political and military measures to prevent a much greater crisis emerging.

Excellencies, as you meet on 23 and 24 March [2011] in
Abuja [Nigeria], we invite you to:

- ask the high representative to be appointed by the
  president of the Commission of the African Union to
  provide a last chance for the outgoing president to
  leave in a dignified manner with guarantees of security,
  and to require an immediate response from him;

- decide on the establishment of a military mission
  whose objective would be to allow the regional community to protect, along with UNOCI [the United Nations Operation in Côte d'Ivoire, a peacekeeping mission tasked to facilitate peace in the Ivory Coast] forces,
  all people residing in Côte d'Ivoire in the very likely
  case of the eruption of massive violence, to support
  military action and decisions which could be taken by
  ECOWAS in accordance with developments in the
  months to come, and help President Ouattara and his

Côte d'Ivoire Overview

Côte d'Ivoire (Ivory Coast) is a developing country on the western coast of Africa. The official capital is Yamoussoukro, but Abidjan is the largest city, the main commercial center, and the location of the Ivorian government and the U.S. embassy. Côte d'Ivoire is a republic whose constitution provides for separate branches of government under a strong president.

The country has experienced continued, periodic episodes of political unrest and violence since 2002, when a failed coup attempt evolved into an armed rebellion that split the country in two. Ivorian President Laurent Gbagbo and New Forces leader Guillaume Soro signed the Ouagadougou Political Agreement (OPA) in March 2007, and a new government was formed with Soro as prime minister. Implementing the accord has been slow and although the political situation has improved, it still has not returned to normal. . . .

Following President Gbagbo's February 12, 2010, dissolution of the Government of Côte d'Ivoire and mandate to Prime Minister Soro to form a new government and a new electoral commission, a period of heightened political unrest led to violence and deaths of opposition protesters. While United Nations (UN) peacekeepers and French military substantially reduced their presence in Côte d'Ivoire in the last two years, both forces remain deployed to safeguard against further violence and instability.

US State Department, 2011.

government to ensure authority over all defence and security forces and to control the entire territory;

- ask the United Nations Security Council to consider emergency measures that could take the form of preventive military actions by UNOCI to more effectively protect civilian populations, such as disabling the mobility of armed elements undertaking indiscriminate attacks with heavy weaponry in Abidjan [the former capital city of Côte d'I'voire];

- ask the Peace and Security Council of the African Union and the UN Security Council to adopt individual sanctions against those who reject the decision of the Peace and Security Council of the African Union dated 10 March 2011, those who are responsible for deliberate attacks on civilians, and those who openly call for violence, or are responsible for broadcast and print media messages inciting hatred and violence.

ECOWAS has played a key role since the beginning of the Ivorian crisis. Its leadership is more important than ever. Since 28 November 2010, Gbagbo's efforts to remain in power no longer leave any doubt about the serious threat that his regime poses to peace and security throughout West Africa. The cost of inaction is much higher now than that of taking strong political and military measures.

"*The solution to the Ivorian crisis doesn't lie in a military intervention, but in the 'natural' implosion of the [Laurent] Gbagbo regime, as the international community is keen on seeing it fall.*"

Nigeria Should Not Intervene in the Ivory Coast Conflict

Alex Engwete

Alex Engwete is a reporter and political commentator. In the following viewpoint, he opposes Nigerian military intervention in the Ivory Coast crisis, even under the auspices of the Economic Community of West African States (ECOWAS), because it could result in severe collateral damage that would discredit the idea of democracy in the region. The author believes that Nigeria should get its own house in order and focus on its own internal conflicts, and not try to throw its weight around in the Ivory Coast. Instead, the ECOWAS should just wait for the situation to resolve itself and rely on the United Nations and French peacekeeping forces to defuse and resolve the situation.

As you read, consider the following questions:

1. Why does the author single out Nigeria and not Ghana?

2. What does the author predict will come of Nigeria's hubris and ambition in West African politics?

3. How does the author characterize Nigerian troops and security forces when left to their own devices?

I recently heard on Radio France Internationale (RFI) a thought-provoking discussion by two members of an extant school of Parisian geostrategists about the increasing irrelevance of wars in solving problems nowadays. In fact, according to one of them, we now live in a POST-MILITARY AGE!

The Efficiency of Military Intervention

This sounds paradoxically counterintuitive as there are so many flash points and armed conflicts of varying intensity around the globe. But the argument is instead to be understood in this wise: With the rise of guerrilla and insurgency capabilities that military invasions by Western powers invariably obtain in their wake, military solutions have become increasingly unsustainable due to the costs in lives, money, time, and (domestic) political capital that quagmires entail. (The unsustainability of military costs, though not elaborated, is however contained in the claim of the French futurologist and one-time president [François] Mitterrand's advisor Jacques Attali that future wars will mostly be waged by mercenaries, now called by the euphemism "military contractors.")

Military victories have become so elusive even for the world's sole superpower despite its several mighty branches and formidable defense budget that (to [Barack] Obama's credit) it now sets its own arbitrary definition and threshold of victory: for example, the withdrawal from Iraq; soon, the drawdown and, ultimately, a "disengagement" from Afghanistan (in effect, an utter fiasco of all COIN [counterinsurgency] doctrines).

The Situation in Côte d'Ivoire

But, the theory of the Parisian geostrategists notwithstanding, large-scale wars and invasions are still likely to occur—as the recent crisis in the Korean peninsula [conflict between North and South Korea] amply demonstrates. What's more, a regional war is about to be waged against Côte d'Ivoire [translated in English as the Ivory Coast] by Nigeria in the coming weeks, with massive U.S. logistical support.

I single out Nigeria because Ghana, the other significant military power within ECOWAS [Economic Community of West African States, an alliance of several African countries], has already ruled out its participation in the projected military adventure and there's a split in the regional organization between hawks and doves.

This being said, the question at issue is whether the Nigerian president has fully considered the basic definition of war that Carl von Clausewitz [a German military theorist] couches in his cautionary maxim: "War is simply the continuation of policy by other means."

The Point of Military Intervention

What exactly is the "policy" that the permanently and firmly capped Goodluck Jonathan wants to achieve in Côte d'Ivoire in the guise of ECOWAS?

If the policy is to enforce "democracy," Jonathan will have to think again and come up with a clear and satisfactory definition of that notion within the context of West Africa. I already showed in my previous posts on this subject, that there is no definable standard of the term in that neighborhood, let alone in the world at large, as the Honduran coup [a 2009 military coup that ousted the sitting president in Honduras] demonstrates. But I'd reiterate as an illustration to flesh up my argument here just two examples I have previously given:

1) Blaise Compraoré, the president of Burkina Faso, has so successfully emptied the notion of democracy of all its substance that he's been clinging to power for more than two decades (thanks to his own definition of democracy);

2) In Niger, a military junta has actually saved democracy by staging a coup against a democratically elected president who was about to subvert democracy by changing the constitution so as to allow him to stand for re-election indefinitely, just like his colleague in Burkina Faso. And the Niger example also shows that there's nothing that guarantees that when the time comes Ouattara wouldn't repeat his predecessor's malpractice.

Would then Nigeria intervene in Côte d'Ivoire again and again?

Charity Starts at Home

Carl von Clausewitz also qualifies his definition of war by saying that:

> "No one starts a war—or rather, no one in his senses ought to do so—without first being clear in his mind what he intends to achieve by that war and how he intends to conduct it."

It is obvious to me that Goodluck Jonathan has taken leave of his "senses" as "democracy," as I have briefly shown, is not a clearly definable notion, let alone an achievable policy goal warranting war in the region. Even in a country with a strong civil society such as Nigeria, democracy is still teetering on the brink of sharia, inter-ethnic and religious violence and terror, as well as a separatist pull in the Niger Delta [an oil-rich region in southern Nigeria]. If anything, that's where Jonathan ought to start his war for democracy, according to the old adage: "Charity starts at home." Besides, the fact that there's not so much of a domestic debate over the advisability of Nigeria starting this war is in itself a commentary on Nigerian democracy.

Who Appointed Nigeria Top Cop?

Closely related to this point is the questionable self-appointment of Nigeria as the "democracy" cop in the regional precinct of West Africa. A self-appointment that shows Nigeria's hubris and ambition at dominating West Africa. I predict that this naked ambition would end up breaking up ECOWAS, preventing further integration within the regional organization, and serving as a deterrent to other African states from joining what they'd perceive as "imperial" regional organizations. . . .

There are also what Clausewitz calls "frictions" (impediments or imponderables) once war starts, as no war unfolds according to plan.

Well, Abidjan [the former capital city in Côte d'Ivoire] and other major cities could fall without much resistance as some anticipate that the Ivorian army might suddenly be incentivized with money to switch sides, and [Laurent] Gbagbo [the incumbent president of Côte d'Ivoire] killed or captured.

Worst-Case Scenarios for Nigeria

But what if "frictions" turn out to be much costlier than anticipated, with, among other developments, a full-blown insurgency that could paralyze the country's economy and government, and get Nigerian troops bogged down in a war of attrition? There's also the dangerous notion being contemplated by some others, of having the northern rebel Forces Nouvelles [New Forces] fight alongside Nigerian troops, just as the Northern Alliance did alongside coalition troops in the invasion of Afghanistan. Left to their own devices, Nigerian troops and security forces are natural-born barbarians renowned for their ruthlessness and their summary executions

The Ivory Coast Conflict

On November 28, 2010, a presidential election runoff vote was held between the incumbent president, Laurent Gbagbo, and former Prime Minister Alassane Ouattara, the two candidates who had won the most votes in a first-round October 31, 2010, poll. Both candidates claim to have won the runoff vote and separately inaugurated themselves as president and formed rival governments. Ouattara bases his victory claim on the UN [United Nations]-certified runoff results announced by Côte d'Ivoire's Independent Electoral Commission (IEC). These show that he won the election with a 54.1% share of votes, against 45.9% for Gbagbo. The international community, including the United States, has endorsed the IEC-announced poll results as accurate and authoritative and demanded that Gbagbo accept them and cede the presidency to Ouattara. Gbagbo, however, appealed the IEC decision to the Ivoirian Constitutional Council, which reviewed and annulled it, proclaiming Gbagbo president, with 51.5% of votes against 48.6% for Ouattara.

The electoral standoff has caused a sharp rise in political tension and violence, resulting in many deaths and human rights abuses, and provoked attacks on UN peacekeepers. The international community has broadly rejected Gbagbo's electoral victory claim and endorsed Ouattara as the legally elected president, and is using diplomatic and financial efforts, personal sanctions, and a military intervention threat to pressure Gbagbo to step aside. Top US officials have attempted to directly pressure Gbagbo to step down, and an existing US ban on bilateral aid has been augmented with visa restrictions and financial sanctions targeting the Gbagbo administration.

Nicolas Cook, "Cote d'Ivoire Post-Election Crisis,"
Congressional Research Service, January 28, 2011.

of civilians; summary executions which did in fact routinely occur when Nigeria participated in ECOMOG [Economic Community of West African States Monitoring Group] forces in Liberia in 1990 and still occur in Nigerian cities every day. Add to that unstable mix the unruly Forces Nouvelles, and you get an explosive mess that would render the military intervention a murderous undertaking.

The solution to the Ivorian crisis doesn't lie in a military intervention, but in the "natural" implosion of the Gbagbo regime, as the international community is keen on seeing it fall. There are already UN [United Nations] and French forces on the ground who, if given the right mandate, are able to make sure that chaos doesn't ensue in the process. Inviting Nigerian soldiers into the imbroglio would result in hefty collateral damage that would discredit democracy being brandished about so menacingly.

> *"Make no mistake: What is happening in Nigeria is a battle of religion."*

There Is Sectarian Violence in Nigeria

Joseph Bottum

Joseph Bottum is an editor at the Weekly Standard *and the editor in chief of* First Things. *In the following viewpoint, he argues that the conflict between Muslims and Christians in Nigeria poses a serious national security threat to the country. Bottum suggests that Nigerians stop denying the true cause of the violence and address the problem realistically and courageously, instead of labeling it an ethnic or economic conflict. He also recommends arming the Christian community to protect itself from Muslim attacks, if the Nigerian security forces are unwilling or unable to do it.*

As you read, consider the following questions:

1. According to the author, what religion has grown dramatically in Nigeria in recent years?

2. How many Nigerian states does the author say adopted Islamic sharia law in 1999?

3. How many Christian churches does the author say have been burned in Nigeria from 2006 to 2010?

Early last Wednesday morning, March 17 [2010], a Muslim mob swept through the Christian villages of Biye and Batem in central Nigeria. At least 13 dead. At least a dozen homes burned. Machetes. Children and pregnant women among the dead. Tongues cut from the corpses. All the usual horrors.

And all the usual responses. The state governor, Jonah Jang, declared . . . that the government is "taking necessary measures and exploring all possible avenues," without having much to say about what those measures and avenues might be. The state police carefully explained that the responsibility for security lies with the military. And the military reacted by issuing a press statement—an extraordinary document which somehow managed both to insist that "but for the timely intervention of troops deployed at the Riyom area, carnages would have been carried out in the two communities" and to admit, a paragraph later, that at least "nine people were killed at Biye while 13 houses were burnt in both communities before the arrival of the troops."

Perhaps such a small number of murders and arsons doesn't count anymore as carnage in Nigeria—which is a sign of how close the nation is to collapse. The attacks on the villages 28 miles south of the state capital of Jos came just ten days after major attacks on three farming villages 3 miles south of Jos that left (according to the BBC) 500 dead and 75 houses burned.

Police who were warned of mobs gathering from out of state more than 24 hours before these attacks of March 7. A security force that didn't even begin to move until two hours after the attacks. And emergency text messages from the governor that didn't go through, a spokesman explained, because of "low batteries" in the cell phones of the leading generals.

This Is Sectarian Violence

Much of this is the incompetence, corruption, and fear of encountering well-armed rebels typical of too many third world militaries. But another factor is at work in Nigeria—for the military police forces are terrified of being perceived as taking sides in the struggles between Christians and Muslims that divide the country.

Make no mistake: What is happening in Nigeria is a battle of religion. Perhaps it has roots in the ancient divide between herdsmen and farmers. Perhaps it echoes some of the old tribal animosities among the Fulani, Berom, Hausa, Tarok, Yoruba, Ibo, and all the rest. And perhaps it is exacerbated by the geographical problems of a nation with an impoverished but politically powerful north and an oil-rich but weak south. One way or another, however, these divisions are now invariably translated into religious terms—and the blood that gets spilled is always in the name of God.

Not that anyone wants to admit it. The conflict has "more to do with disputes over access to natural resources than religion," insisted John Onaiyekan, the Catholic archbishop of Abuja. It is "fueled more by ethnic, social, and economic problems than religion," said the former president, Olusegun Obasanjo, according to a CNN report.

A Government in Denial

But even while they make these statements, you can hear the wishful tone—the overriding desire to make untrue the truth they all actually know. If it's about corruption, or politics, or social problems, then it has a cause and perhaps someone to blame. But if it is about religion, what then should they do?

The population of Nigeria is almost exactly half Muslim (mostly in the north) and half Christian (mostly in the south), but the division is not stable. Christianity has grown dramatically in recent decades—the nearly complete Christianizing of sub-Saharan Africa in the 20th century is one of the greatest stories of conversion in history—and the new Christians of Nigeria have no desire to stop their advance. Islam lives badly with other religions even where it is confidently dominant, and in Nigeria, it feels insecure and defensive, with the nation's proselytizing energy arrayed against it.

There may have been more politics than religion behind the adoption of Islamic sharia law by 12 northern states in 1999; the demagogues were out in force at the time, and in Zamfara, the first state to take the plunge, the governor was desperately looking for an issue he could ride. But the reason that sharia could be such an issue—the cause of its political salience—was the deep, existential insecurity from which the Islamic population of Nigeria suffers.

They can feel themselves slowly losing—in Nigeria, almost uniquely among countries with a large Muslim population—and it should not be surprising that they lash out against the missionaries who come up to proselytize in the northern states and against the Christian communities in the central states like Plateau, with its small villages around the religiously divided city of Jos.

Violence on Both Sides of the Conflict

The Christians are hardly blameless. Accurate figures of what is called the Yelwa massacre are impossible to find; Caroline Cox of the Humanitarian Aid Relief Trust has accused Islamic propagandists of systematic exaggeration: "A consistent pattern has emerged" in all these clashes, in which "Muslim militants" take all the corpses, Christian and Muslim alike, to mosques, "where they are photographed and released to the media, creating the impression that these are Muslim victims." Nonetheless, there seems no doubt that Christians brutally attacked Muslims in the central Nigerian town of Yelwa in 2004.

But the far more usual pattern is one of Islamic attacks, with a consistent attempt by the Western media to find moral equivalence, or even to blame the Christians for provoking the

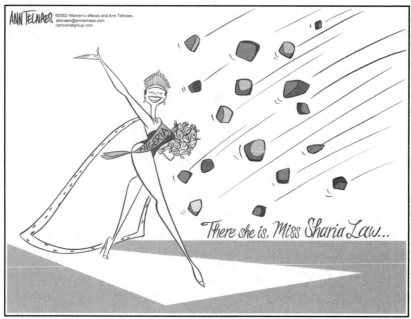

There she is, Miss Sharia Law...

attacks. Predictable "reprisal" and "revenge" for Christian violence, the *Los Angeles Times* sniffed after the March 7 murders.

This will not do. Over 300 Christian churches have been burned in Nigeria over the last four years. Jos has become a war zone, and the opening blow is almost always from the Islamic side. The September 2001 battle—1,000 dead—began when a Muslim mob attacked a Christian woman for crossing a mosque's grounds during prayer. The November 2008 riot—400 dead—grew from a Muslim crowd's violent protest of local election results. And the January 2010 clash—200 dead—started, according to the state police commissioner, when Muslims set a Catholic church on fire.

Conflict Is a National Security Threat

The political instability of Nigeria remains an open threat to the communities in the central states. The vice president, a Christian named Goodluck Jonathan, was appointed acting president by the legislature on February 9, after two and half months of absence by the Muslim president, Umaru Yar'Adua, who was receiving medical treatment in Saudi Arabia. Yar'Adua reportedly returned to Nigeria on February 24. No one other than his wife has claimed to have seen him, and rumors abound that he is in a coma. But his alleged presence in the country clouds the political situation, and Jonathan's response came on March 17, when he dismissed the entire 42-member cabinet Yar'Adua had assembled—an act for which it is not clear he has constitutional authority.

Then, the next day, Jonathan ordered home the Nigerian ambassador to Libya, after Muammar Gaddafi called for dividing Nigeria into two countries, Muslim and Christian, in order to "stop bloodshed and burning of places of worship." That's not the nuttiest idea the Libyan leader has ever suggested, but it resonated badly among Nigerians who remember the civil war that followed the secession of Biafra in the late 1960s. It would require Nigeria's Christians, moreover, to surrender to the ungentle power of permanent Muslim authority their small but growing communities in the north. And why should they agree to that?

This political confusion could easily issue in a military coup and subsequent civil war—which, given the way all conflict in Nigeria quickly translates into religious battle, would mean yet more sectarian violence. In the face of that threat, who could want a distribution of weapons to ethnic and religious communities? But when government fails, people must assume the functions of government.

If the Nigerian authorities are so frozen that they cannot safeguard their citizens—if the villages are to suffer, again and again, all the usual horrors—then there will be only two things for the churches, both in Nigeria and abroad, to do: Arm the Christian communities and damn those whose failures made it necessary.

> *"The reason these conflicts turn deadly in Nigeria is not any greater degree of religious animosity there than elsewhere, however, much exists."*

The Conflict in Central Nigeria Is Economic, Not Sectarian

Peter Cunliffe-Jones

Peter Cunliffe-Jones is an editor at Agence France-Presse news agency and the author of My Nigeria: Five Decades of Independence. *In the following viewpoint, he maintains that the origin of the violence that has erupted in Jos, the capital city of the Plateau state in central Nigeria, is economic, not religious in nature. Cunliffe-Jones reports that Muslims and Christians are fighting about the diminishing access to land, and the skirmishes turn into deadly conflict because of the government's slow and ineffective response to the problem.*

As you read, consider the following questions:

1. How many Nigerians died in Jos in the 2001 fighting, according to the author?

2. How many Nigerians does the author say died during fighting in the same region in 2008?

3. When does the author say that Islam spread over much of northern Nigeria?

Even by Nigerian standards, the city of Jos, which was the scene of hundreds of killings this weekend [March 5–8, 2010], is a disputatious place.

In a country where bloodshed is all too frequent, the Tin City, set in among the hills of Nigeria's central Plateau region, has gained an unenviable reputation for bloody violence in recent years—a symbol to the outside world of the supposed enmity between the country's Muslim and Christian populations.

Violence in the Tin City

Many hundreds—some say, up to 2,000—died there in fighting between Muslims and Christians in 2001, when I was reporting on Nigeria for the AFP [Agence France-Presse] news agency. Hundreds more died in new fighting in 2008, and hundreds again died in January and this weekend.

To many who report on Africa from a distance, these outbursts of violence are taken as a sign of a "fragile country" on the verge of breaking apart between its mainly Muslim north and mainly Christian south. In fact, the picture is more complex.

For a country where some cities date back over 1,000 years, Jos is a relatively recent settlement, established in 1915, 15 years after colonial rule was declared in the region. Even then, the population was cosmopolitan and the political situation complex. Muslim rule had been established over much of northern Nigeria in the early 19th century, but had never quite extended into the hilly Middle Belt region. After the British arrived, the discovery of vast reserves of tin led to an

Sectarian Violence in Nigeria's Middle Belt

In May 2009, the U.S. Commission on International Religious Freedom recommended that Nigeria be classified as a "Country of Particular Concern" [CPC] for religious freedom violations. . . . According to the commission, as many as 12,000 Nigerians have been killed since 1999 in sectarian violence, and the commissioners based the CPC recommendation on their belief that the country is tolerating this violence. According to their 2010 report, "Not a single criminal, Muslim or Christian, has been convicted and sentenced in Nigeria's ten years of religious violence. Therein lies the problem. The Nigerian government and judicial system have so far been unwilling or unable to protect either side."

The report cites hundreds of recent deaths in sectarian violence in Jos, the capital of Plateau State in central Nigeria, which sits between the predominately Muslim north and Christian south.

Violence between communities in this "Middle Belt" in the past decade reflects tensions that are not only religious, but also ethnic, and which are exacerbated by some local politicians. These tensions stem from a competition over resources—land, education, government jobs—between ethnic groups classified as settlers or "indigene" (original inhabitants of the state), a designation that conveys political and economic benefits. . . . According to Human Rights Watch, over 1,000 were killed in intercommunal fighting and targeted killings in Plateau State in 2010.

Lauren Ploch, "Nigeria: Elections and Issues for Congress," Congressional Research Service, April 1, 2011.

influx of migrants from the mainly Christian south, coming to join an indigenous mainly animist population, and Muslims from further north.

The Root of the Conflict

Certainly, religion is one of the many dividing lines in Jos and elsewhere in Nigeria. But it is not the main one.

In Jos, as elsewhere, the cause of fighting has more often been the struggle for resources than it has religion. In Jos, my AFP colleague Aminu Abubakar reports that the original cause of the latest clash was the alleged theft of cattle, blamed by a group of settler-farmers on a group of cattle herders. Often the fighting in the north is between the semi-nomadic cattle herders (who happen to be mostly Muslim) and settler-farmers (who happen to be mostly Christian), fighting about the diminishing access to land.

"For all those who will go out and fight their Muslim or Christian brothers on the streets, there are many more (Nigerians) who will take them into their homes to protect them, when fighting breaks out," a Nigerian Islamic law student once told me, attending an animist festival in the south.

A Failure of Law Enforcement and Government Response

The reason these conflicts turn deadly in Nigeria is not any greater degree of religious animosity there than elsewhere, however, much exists. The reason is poor government: one that fails to send in troops early enough to quell trouble when it flares and never jails those responsible when it is over. Mediation of disputes is too often left to others, too.

Religion may indeed be a dividing line in Nigeria. But politics, problem solving and resource management hold the key to peace in Nigeria.

> "In the past 50 years this so-called
> Nigeria's unity has been maintained
> with the blood of millions of innocent
> children, women and men."

Nigeria Should Be Divided Along Sectarian Lines

Osita Ebiem

Osita Ebiem is a Biafran political commentator. In the following viewpoint, he derides the culture of appeasement and deceit in Nigeria that allows political and religious officials to deny that the violence that threatens to tear the country apart is predominantly religious in nature. Ebiem suggests that the original founding of Nigeria was done because of British administrative convenience and does not reflect the reality of the country's ethnic, social, and religious situation. He recommends that Nigeria be divided into six different countries, bringing an end to the violence and suffering of Nigerian citizens.

As you read, consider the following questions:

1. Who does the author say was responsible for the 2010 attacks in Jos?

2. When did Nigeria become independent from England?

3. According to the author, how many different ethnic groups are there in Nigeria?

On the 24th of December, 2010 about nine bombs exploded in the city of Jos, Plateau State. The toll is put at 80 dead and 109 wounded. These deaths and mayhem are unnecessary, should not have happened and should never happen again. Every social problem can be solved when the people are willing, honest and sincere. Truth, honesty and sincerity are the bedrocks on which social justice is founded. But unfortunately truth is the scarcest commodity in the Nigerian state or among its inhabitants. In fact the country and its people are allergic to truth; they abhor it.

A Culture of Dishonesty

Nigeria and Nigerians are the greatest lie and liars of all time. It is a country with the culture of lies, dishonesty and deceit. Nigeria as a country is a lie and it has continually lived up to its founding purpose. This Nigerian-culture-of-lie is true no matter how highly or lowly placed a Nigerian is. A Nigerian's social, political and religious or any other status does not really make a difference, he tells and lives a lie all the same.

After the cowardly explosions in Jos and the killings in Maiduguri [the capital city of the Borno state in Nigeria], the Jama'atu Ahlus Sunnah Lidda'awati Wal Jihad, also known as Boko Haram, an Islamic fundamentalist/terrorist group, claimed responsibility for the murders and destructions.

Before the attack rumor had been rife in the state that there would be some very deadly Islamic jihadist attacks in the city of Jos during the Christmas period. Then the time came and the attacks were carried out as rumored on Friday the 24th of December, 2010. By the following Monday Boko Haram which is a local cell of the Osama bin Laden's international al-Qaeda terrorist group claimed responsibility.

What followed is what is indeed wrong with Nigeria; the culture of lie and dishonesty, irrespective of a Nigerian's station in life and society. By virtue of being the president of the Christian Association of Nigeria (CAN) Pastor Ayo Oritsejafor is the head of all Christians in Nigeria. And in the characteristic of Nigeria and all Nigerians he came out in the press after a meeting with some Islamic leaders and with a straight face, said that the acts were not carried out by the radical Islamic group who claimed responsibility. He said it was by a faceless politically motivated group. In Nigeria no matter how obvious things are they are shamefacedly distorted and it is business as usual afterwards. Nobody is ever held responsible for lies or deceits because the state itself is a lie.

This head of all Christians in Nigeria was only short of saying that the attacks of both the Maiduguri churches and worshippers, of same day, where six people were killed and the Jos Christmas Eve bombs were actually committed by Christians against fellow Christians and their places of worship.

The Politics of Pacifism

On his own position as the governor of Plateau State—he is also a pastor as well as the governor—Pastor Jonah Jang said that since Muslims were also killed in the attacks then they were politically motivated. He would have also said that it was not committed by the radicalized Muslim jihadists who had consistently unleashed mayhem in the state as long as anyone can remember. Logically what follows is that those who are in position of responsibility in Nigeria are either oblivious of the dynamics of the societies they are supposed to oversee or they are outright liars. And because the country is a blatant lie it is easy to conclude that the later is the truth.

Some people have argued that these people in positions of influence are only playing the sordid politics of appeasement and pacifism. Or some believe that these unconscionable leaders actually benefit directly from the situations to the detriment of the people they are leading.

Recent Terrorist and Sectarian Violence in Côte d'Ivoire

In 2010, alleged Boko Haram members claimed responsibility for bombings in the country. A bomb exploded December 31, 2010, near a busy Abuja "fish bar," killing several people and injuring many others. On December 24, 2010, alleged Boko Haram members detonated several explosive devices in Jos, Plateau State, and conducted attacks against police and others in Maiduguri, Borno State, leading to significant casualties and property loss. In October 2010, Boko Haram members attacked various Nigerian government security personnel and facilities, government officials, and authority figures in northeastern Bauchi and Borno States. On October 1, 2010, two car bombs detonated near Eagle Square in downtown Abuja during Independence Day celebrations, killing ten and wounding many others. A Movement [for the Emancipation of] the Niger Delta (MEND) spokesperson claimed responsibility for this attack, while most former MEND militants publicly disavowed any links. Since then, this MEND spokesperson threatened further bombings in Abuja. In September 2010, over 150 members of the Boko Haram extremist religious sect escaped from prison in northeast Bauchi, some of whom may be participating in Boko Haram attacks in other parts of the country. Since March 2010, five improvised explosive devices (IEDs) have detonated in the Niger Delta region with one to three reported casualties.

US State Department, April 15, 2011.

When in 1914 the British government merged the north and south of what is today's Nigeria it was done for their administrative convenience and not out of any honesty of purpose or any parameter that reflected the reality of the indigenous peoples' cultures and way of life. When in 1960 the same Britain handed the power of the so-called independent Nigeria to the northerners it was through some very blatant and dishonest process.

And when in 1967 the British once again ganged up with Nigeria and other countries such as the Soviet Union (today's Russia), Saudi Arabia and the rest of the Arab world with Egypt supplying combatants to commit the worst kind of genocide on the African continent on the Igbo/Biafrans it was based on a false premise. The British were taking orders from the Saudi princes and being manipulated just like they did when Nigeria's [Umaru] Yar'Adua was already dead in Saudi Arabia and the British Broadcasting Corporation, BBC, was busy airing a concocted news interview with the dead as living. They fed the world lies again about Nigeria because it is not their children or countrymen who die in the genocides.

Unity Is a Sham

With the passage of time, because the foundation has always been wrong, the Nigerian state and all its citizens have come to perfect this culture of lie and falsehood such that the natural offsprings are such things like genocide, fanatical Islamic jihadism, graft and corruption and unbelief in truths. There are over 250 different ethnic groups in Nigeria with distinct and in certain cases irreconcilable cultural differences. And based on this fact, Nigeria should not have been one country and must not remain one country. It must be divided into at least six separate countries. In a referendum the people must be allowed to choose either to continue as one country or go their separate ways.

In the past 50 years this so-called Nigeria's unity has been maintained with the blood of millions of innocent children, women and men. In the Nigeria's genocide in Biafra alone 3.1

million Biafrans were murdered. And since the end of that genocidal Biafra war in 1970 the unnecessary murders and destructions have continued unabated purely along the cultural divides of the various societies in the enclave. The population has remained restive and the real people who suffer the pains of this senseless culture of lie and dishonesty want an immediate end to their suffering. They are tired of the untruths and the politics of appeasement by their so-called leaders and the dictation of outsiders who are forcing down their throats the doctrine of deathly-unity because it is not the children of the outsiders that die in these wanton jihadisms.

> *"People from the northern, eastern and western parts of the country should be able to live and work together in any part of the country without seeing themselves first as Hausa-Fulani, Ibo or Yoruba, but as Nigerians."*

National Integration Should Be a Top Priority in Nigeria

Sam Adesua

Sam Adesua is a columnist for the Nigerian Tribune. *In the following viewpoint, he states that the lack of any comprehensive national integration programs in Nigeria has resulted in a fragmented and suspicious society whose citizens often turn to violence to solve their problems. Earlier attempts to bring together the ethnically diverse group of citizens who make up Nigeria have ended up in failure because they have not addressed the cause of the problem. Adesua contends that government officials have to make national integration a top priority if they are serious about ending the senseless sectarian violence that plagues the nation.*

As you read, consider the following questions:

1. How many people does the author estimate have been killed by the violence in Jos?

2. According to Adesua, how many ethnic groups coexist in Nigeria?

3. Who called the unification of Nigeria "the mistake of 1914"?

The madness that has decimated Jos since early this year continued unabated and even assumed a more frightening dimension at this tail end of the year. Latest reports showed that last weekend [December 24, 2010], demented sadists in Jos, the Plateau State capital, again, employed explosives to swell the number of hapless and innocent Nigerians dispatched to their untimely graves by more than 30.

A National Shame

We have focussed on this madness earlier in this column. Since the next victims of the seeming endless and senseless carnage are still in the dark about their pending catastrophic end, it is pertinent to reiterate our candid view on the madness as reproduced below.

The resonant killings in Jos, the Plateau State capital, and the suburbs have become a national embarrassment, not only to the state governor and the peaceful people of the state, but also to all Nigerians. No fewer than 1,000 innocent people and properties worth billions of naira [Nigerian currency] had been consumed by the senseless carnage. The savagery has attracted international attention. Many Nigerians are, however, of the view that the carnage must have been sponsored by some elites who, for quintessentially ulterior motive, view every problem in the country with prejudiced ethnic and/or religious lenses.

I guess that the alleged veiled sponsors of such malady themselves must by now be embarrassed by the level of wanton destruction of lives and properties of hapless and inno-cent Nigerians resident in the once peaceful and highly attrac-tive environment. Some of the residents who had managed to survive the mindless killings had lost their means of human survival.

Moammar Gadhafi's Solution

It was on the platform of this malady that Libya's life presi-dent, Moammar Gadhafi, who is incurably contemptuous of anything Nigeria and even black Africa, suggested the balkani-sation [dividing into smaller units] of the country, ostensibly along religious lines.

Although many panels and committees have hitherto worked and are still working on the resolution of the Jos crisis and related ones elsewhere, the problem has become seem-ingly intractable, because it appears that the focus has always been on only the symptom rather than the cause of the prob-lem. At the end of the day, an appeal would go to the feuding parties to embrace peace by seeing themselves as compatriots. But their orientation or upbringing is quite antithetic to this meaningless sociopolitical sermon. Thus, after each crisis, a repeat of the carnage would just be waiting to be unveiled. This has been the pattern over the years in the country as ob-viated by the seemingly unending Jos intermittent madness.

It is pertinent to emphasise that Nigeria is a conglomera-tion of more than 200 divergent and often discordant ethnic groups.

No Historic Effort at Integration

Unfortunately, since "the mistake of 1914" (as Sir Ahmadu Bello, the late Sardauna of Sokoto [a Nigerian politician] would want everyone to see the amalgamation of the northern and southern parts of Nigeria), there has never been any con-scious effort by any of the past leaders towards national inte-gration in the country.

The sociopolitical surgery done by the British imperialists was meant for mere administrative convenience for the maximum exploitation of the emerging nation. In other words, British imperialists had no concern for a stable polity beyond the years of imperialists' plunder of the country which, of course, was also part of their neo-colonial strategy during the days of colonialism.

Thus, the issue of national integration was never part of the agenda of the colonialists.

Therefore, the seemingly intractable problem of national integration in Nigeria has become glaring even to the blind. This has created very potent centrifugal forces within the polity over the years. These forces became very active and glaring in the various political crises that culminated in the 30 months fratricidal civil war which almost put an end to Nigeria as a corporate entity.

The awareness of this by the nation's decision makers reflect in various palliative measures put in place which, however, have not only been underscoring the problem of national integration, but often added some complexities that exacerbated it.

The Federal Character Phenomenon

Take for instance the issue of federal character, which is one of the palliative measures aimed at addressing the symptoms of the problem of national integration. It is a truism that this measure has created more problems than it tried to solve. It has been the source of some inter-ethnic acrimony in the country. In some cases, the federal character phenomenon had sidelined merit (if not totally sacrificed) for the ascendancy of mediocrity.

In Nigeria for instance, because of the accident of birth place, a student from Imo State, for example, may not be admitted into the Nigerian university for not scoring enough marks, while his counterpart from Sokoto, who scored the same or even lower marks, may be admitted. The truth of the matter is that the two young men cannot see themselves as true compatriots.

This same problem explains the reason somebody with a degree in Islamic studies could be employed as a banker on the platform of his place of birth, while another Nigerian with a degree in accountancy or banking and finance, because of the accident of birth place, would be denied such opportunity and would be made to roam the streets hopelessly. How do we expect such two people to see themselves as one? This is part of the roots of acrimony, mutual distrust or even arrant hatred, especially on the platform of ethnic leaning.

The Importance of National Integration

The solution to this problem lies in conscious efforts towards national integration by Nigerian leaders. People from the northern, eastern and western parts of the country should be able to live and work together in any part of the country without seeing themselves first as Hausa-Fulani, Ibo or Yoruba, but as Nigerians. This is the only thing that can end mutual suspicion and arrant hatred based on ethnic or sectional leaning. This is the only way to avoid the senseless killings in Jos and such madness elsewhere in Nigeria.

| "Thus far, the Nigerian government has displayed paralysis and indifference when it comes to resolving the conflict in the Niger Delta."

The Niger Delta Conflict Requires Strong Leadership from Nigerian Leaders and the International Community

Kelly Campbell

Kelly Campbell is a senior program assistant in the Center for Conflict Analysis and Prevention at the United States Institute of Peace. In the following viewpoint, Campbell observes that the Nigerian government has displayed ambivalence and paralysis when it comes to initiating an effective peace agreement in the Niger Delta. A more promising approach to negotiating peace in the troubled region is a process bringing together all parties involved in the conflict, including government officials, citizens of the Niger Delta, militants, and representatives of leading oil companies that do business there. Also essential is the participa-

tion of the international community, especially the United States, England, and the United Nations, who can play a vital support- ing role in the peace process.

As you read, consider the following questions:

1. According to the author, how much did militant attacks diminish oil production in the Niger Delta in 2008?

2. Who does the author believe uses militia groups for their own political and economic purposes?

3. What does Campbell think is the first step in the Niger Delta peace process?

The conflict in the Niger Delta has posed a fundamental domestic challenge to Nigerian security for more than a decade. Despite pledges to address continued instability in the delta, the administration of Nigerian President Umaru Yar'Adua has not yet initiated a process to resolve the politi- cal, economic and security problems in the region. Oil pro- duction continues to diminish as a result of militant attacks, and is currently 20 to 25 percent below capacity. Meanwhile, militia members in the Niger Delta continue to engage in criminal activities such as kidnapping and oil bunkering [the process of filling oil into a ship's tanks] to maximize profits for themselves and their political patrons.

Oil bunkering and general instability in the region com- pound energy problems abroad, reducing supply and driving up the cost of oil in global markets. Nigeria is currently the fourth-largest supplier of oil to the United States; in March 2008 alone, the U.S. imported 1.154 million barrels per day from Nigeria. . . .

Instability in the Niger Delta: Background and Major Issues

The conflict in the Niger Delta has its roots in the increasing protests of the region's communities against their political, economic and environmental disenfranchisement. The Movement for the Survival of the Ogoni People (MOSOP), launched in 1990, was the first group to gain international attention for their grievances against the Nigerian government and regional oil companies. MOSOP's goals included increased local control over resources and more equitable development. MOSOP also sought the resolution of fishing and fanning issues that arose from the environmental effects of oil extraction, such as oil spills, acid rain and soil degradation. Protection of human rights became another demand after peaceful protests by the Ogoni people were met with arrests, repression and violence from the military regime of General Sani Abacha. The Ogoni movement inspired a host of similar organizing efforts in the region, particularly among the Ijaw.

The center of protests and political activism then shifted to western states in the Niger Delta, particularly Bayelsa and Delta States, where the Itsekiri, Urhobo, Ilaje and Ijaw communities began mobilizing over boundary and resource issues. The Ijaw in particular demanded accountability from regional political officials and a greater voice in the region's affairs. Their demands were outlined in the Kaiama Declaration, released in December 1998, which called for the immediate withdrawal of the military from Ijaw areas and the cessation of oil production if equitable control over these resources was not returned to the oil-producing communities. Clashes between Ijaw groups and the Nigerian government led to the imposition of emergency rule in late 1998 and early 1999. Tensions culminated in the Odi massacre in November 1999, in which the Nigerian military killed dozens of citizens.

After a brief lull in violence, the conflict in the Niger Delta escalated in 2002 and 2003, particularly during and after the election process in 2003. Three overarching and interconnected problems contribute to continued regional instability: lack of good governance; lack of social and economic development; and increased militarization.

Lack of Good Governance

The Nigerian state lacks political legitimacy at all levels of government because of chronically flawed elections, the most blatant of which were the rigged elections of 2007. The lack of legitimacy is more pronounced in the Niger Delta, which suffers from what one speaker called a "striking lack of democracy." The region has never had credible elections since the military returned to the barracks in 1999. In both the 2003 and 2007 elections, voter turnout in the Niger Delta was extremely low, on average less than five percent. Gang members on the payroll of politicians and party officials intimidated the few voters who showed up at polling stations, and in many areas no elections were held at all—yet the official election results reported more than 90 percent turnout in some states. In Bayelsa State, despite single-digit voter participation in the 2003 election witnessed by both domestic and international observers, the official final tally amounted to 123 percent participation. During the 2007 elections, Nigerian officials reported results for polling stations that were never even opened in Rivers State.

The federal government has also failed to provide goods and services to the people of the Niger Delta, who experience terrible poverty despite living in the region that produces the vast majority of Nigeria's wealth. Widespread corruption and lack of transparency in detailing how oil money is allocated and spent at the state level further erode the people's trust in the government. Equally important, neither the government nor the oil companies have adequately addressed environmental problems such as gas flaring and oil spills. Finally, the Nigerian government has not provided adequate security to communities in the Niger Delta. With few exceptions, the government has allowed gangs and militias, some of which are funded by local politicians and party officials, to run rampant. Violence between rival gangs—particularly in the aftermath of the 2003 and 2007 elections—has resulted in the deaths of dozens of innocent civilians. Even when security forces have been deployed to the Niger Delta, they have also committed atrocities against civilians, and some officers have been engaged in corruption and the illegal oil trade.

Lack of Social and Economic Development

Little substantive progress has been made in addressing development issues or revenue allocation in the Niger Delta. The region continues to lack adequate social services, viable employment opportunities or economic growth and development. Although in 2006 two-thirds of the militia members and leaders surveyed by Academic Associates PeaceWorks said they would take advantage of training or jobs if they were available, the dearth of such opportunities contributes to the decision of youths to join militias for economic gain. Profiteering from oil bunkering and the kidnapping of oil workers presents a lucrative and increasingly popular alternative, especially since the youth lack any sense of ownership of, participation in or benefit from the oil industry. This virtual exclusion of local individuals or companies from employment opportunities in the oil and gas sectors has led to anger, alienation and aggression. It has also contributed to the steady supply of youth who are willing to join gangs and militias.

Militarization of the Niger Delta

Militia groups in the region have proliferated, often sustained by government and party officials who use the militias for their own political and economic purposes. Groups such as the Movement for the Emancipation of the Niger Delta (MEND), which was organized in 2006, function as a loose network of gangs rather than a coherent organization. They lack a common political agenda or political wings that could participate in a negotiation process. While some groups possess legitimate grievances and goals, they also engage in criminal activities that lead to the continuation of the conflict—by doing the bidding of the politicians and others who pay them, the militia members perpetuate the governance system that contributes to the region's problems.

The militias have become increasingly violent, both toward one another and toward civilians. Kidnapping victims now include not just oil workers, but also children and other people who are not associated with the oil industry. An influx of small arms and more sophisticated weapons into the Niger Delta from regional and international markets has led to the increased arming of the militias. They are now nearly evenly matched with the Nigerian military, which was dispatched to the region in 2003 and maintains a significant presence there. The result has been a stalemate. Politicians in the Niger Delta who fund the militias retain the lion's share of illegally sourced wealth and are able to sustain their activities with minimal losses, raising enough revenue to pay off their patronage networks and militias. Politicians in Abuja [the capital city of Nigeria] offer plans for peace without taking action, doing little to alter the status quo.

The Way Forward: The Role of Nigeria and the International Community

Thus far, the Nigerian government has displayed paralysis and indifference when it comes to resolving the conflict in the Niger Delta. Indeed, Abuja has shown little interest in launching a serious political dialogue process that will address the fundamental issues. However, one speaker argued that a window of opportunity for launching a political dialogue has opened. President Yar'Adua's compromised victory in the 2007 elections diminished his political legitimacy, and over the past year he has worked to earn support and build political alliances. If the Nigerian Supreme Court upholds his victory in the 2007 election, Yar'Adua may feel emboldened to implement his vision for Nigeria, including a peace plan for the Niger Delta. His administration is planning a conference during the summer of 2008 to launch what may be an ambitious peace process, but already many of the key regional stakeholders have not been invited, prompting some militias to threaten anyone from their areas who tries to attend.

Any credible peace process must involve all parties to the conflict, including representatives of the government, the communities of the Niger Delta, the militants and the leading oil companies in the region. A framework for discussion, a forum for articulating grievances and a well-developed agenda are all needed to begin a negotiation process that will lead to a comprehensive solution of the relevant political, economic and security problems. In order to organize and oversee this process, a comprehensive, unified facilitator with regular access to President Yar'Adua will be essential. A federal government task force of the key ministers and oil parastatals that can make decisions and respond quickly to the needs of the peace process would also be of great benefit.

The process must first deal with the governors, party officials and powerful national actors who have established small fiefdoms in the Niger Delta. These potential spoilers have the most to lose in a more legitimate and accountable political system. An elite-targeted negotiation should be conducted in parallel with a public consultation process that engages communities directly, given the lack of accountability of local politicians. Second, jump-starting development projects could provide opportunities for local organizations to play leadership roles, giving the Niger Delta communities a stake in the peace process and convincing them that the government is serious. Discussions about localized resource control and a new formula for allocating resources must also be on the agenda: A principal demand of opposition groups is that the 13 percent of oil and gas revenue that state governments currently receive from the federal government be increased—some argue to as high as 50 percent. Political leaders from other regions sharply disagree, promising a difficult negotiation that will also have to engage the National Assembly in order to amend the revenue formula. National action will also be required for election reform, which is a desperate need for all Nigerians, but is particularly acute in the Niger Delta. Finally, the government will need to play a demonstrable security role. While unleashing the military in the Niger Delta would be counterproductive, the government must provide security for citizens by reining in the militias, perhaps through provisional cease-fire arrangements until a more permanent agreement is reached.

The Role of the International Community

Although the onus to resolve the conflict in the Niger Delta must be on the Nigerian government, the Yar'Adua administration's inaction to date indicates that external pressure must be continued for any kind of problem-solving process to begin. The international community, particularly the U.S. [United States] and the U.K. [United Kingdom], could do a great deal to support a Nigerian-led political dialogue once the Yar'Adua government demonstrates serious initiative. The U.S. and the U.K. are already cooperating closely and quietly encouraging the Nigerians to move swiftly, but they will also have to work to coordinate productive responses from Western oil companies if a comprehensive peace process gets under way. The United Nations [UN] could also play a supporting role with mediation assistance, development aid and environmental cleanup. One speaker suggested the establishment of a contact group that would include the U.N., U.S., U.K. and perhaps China, as well as nongovernmental organizations within the U.S. This group could support a Nigerian-led mediation process with funding and advice, and could lead an effort to control the importation of weapons into the region.

The conflict in the Niger Delta continues to challenge both the Nigerian government and the international community. On the domestic front, one speaker noted that the strategy for moving forward involves an inherent contradiction regarding the nature of federalism in Nigeria. While more localized resource control and democratic policies are needed in the Niger Delta, the federal government's ability to play a more constructive role in establishing security and making governors more accountable is equally important. To date, the international community has deferred to the Nigerian government's insistence that it will handle the matter internally. However, the international community also has a stake in helping to resolve this conflict: The problems in the Niger Delta also destabilize global markets, especially as the price of oil continues to rise. Bringing peace and stability to the region will require the Yar'Adua administration to fulfill its own promises of launching credible peace and development processes, supported by the cooperation of the international community.

> "Yet insecurity in the Niger Delta is a problem not only for the Nigerian government. It is a problem for the United States and the wider world as well."

Oil Companies Must Provide Local Citizens More Control over the Oil Resources in the Niger Delta

Judith Burdin Asuni

Judith Burdin Asuni is a visiting scholar for African studies at Johns Hopkins University's School of Advanced International Studies. In the following viewpoint, she outlines several steps the Nigerian government, oil companies, and the international community can take to alleviate militant activity in the Niger Delta. Asuni underscores the need for oil companies to give the people in the region more control over oil resources—a main grievance of the armed militant groups. This action will likely decrease violence and sabotage of oil equipment and pipelines that disrupts oil production and drains resources. Asuni also asserts the need for the federal government to keep its promises to improve the economic well-being of the people in the Niger Delta.

As you read, consider the following questions:

1. According to the author, how many barrels of oil a day has disruption by militants forced down oil production in the Niger Delta?

2. How will fingerprinting technology help the Nigerian government trace stolen oil?

3. Why does the author recommend that the US government engage more with Nigeria?

Policy Implications

Previous Initiatives

The challenges of finding policy solutions for the problems of the Niger Delta should not be underestimated. The Nigerian government is faced with a damaging low-level insurrection fought by a confusing array of highly motivated armed groups, aided in part by a population angered at their continued exclusion from the economic benefits they had been promised when the oil companies moved in. In addition, disruption by militants has forced down oil production by about one million barrels per day and anything up to 300,000 additional barrels per day through criminal networks with links to members of Nigeria's own security forces and politicians. These are matters of grave concern, both for Nigeria and the United States, which until recently has imported approximately one million barrels of Nigerian oil per day. Yet so far, both the domestic and international responses to the problems of the Niger Delta have been halfhearted and ineffective.

In the Niger Delta itself, various peace plans have been negotiated for the individual states, to little effect. The peace agreement reached in Rivers State in 2004 fell apart, mainly because the disarmament process was flawed and there was insufficient political will to make it succeed. The author played a role in bringing the militant leaders, Asari and Ateke, to meet with President Obasanjo in Abuja in October 2004 and then went to Rivers State to help consolidate the peace agreement. There was a federal government committee, chaired by Governor Odili, that oversaw the disarmament process. Unfortunately, the committee decided to pay cash for weapons, which was simply used to purchase more weapons. The author also worked with the Rivers State rehabilitation committee, which was set up to help transition militants back to normal life. While the first few technical skills-training programs to emerge from this process were focused on the ex-militants, the programs were gradually taken over by the politicians, who used them as a source of patronage for their friends and relatives. While the 2004 Rivers State peace agreement broke down due to broken promises on the part of government, the current governor of Rivers State has refused to engage in a peace process at all. Chibuike Rotimi Amaechi has said that he will not negotiate with "criminals." Instead, more soldiers have been sent to the area, with mixed results.

In Bayelsa State, the peace process that began in December 2007 was a sham. The major signatory is the head of central MEND, Boyloaf, who has simply carried on with business as usual. Although he and his friends have maintained relative peace in Bayelsa State, they have engaged in violence elsewhere, such as the summer 2008 attack on Bonga and their participation in the oil war in Rivers State in September 2008. Until recently, the state government's strategy involved paying both the militants and the military to maintain the peace within its borders. In spring 2009, Governor Timipre Sylva announced that he would no longer pay the militants.

By contrast, the peace process in Delta State has been moderately successful. A waterways security committee, established in May 2007, includes members of some militant groups and has managed to alleviate some of the violence in the region. In addition, several youth leaders have been offered positions in the state government.

At the federal level, there has been plenty of talk and some new initiatives but little in the way of concrete results. The Niger Delta Development Commission (NDDC), set up by former president Obasanjo, was from the outset mired in corruption and undermined by incompetence. President Yar'Adua established a technical committee in late 2008 to study all previous reports on the Niger Delta and plan a strategy. Its findings are now in the hands of another committee for further consideration. The president also established a ministry of the Niger Delta in December 2008 and appointed two ministers to deal specifically with the problems of the region. It is too early to judge these initiatives' effectiveness.

Turning to the international level, the Gulf of Guinea Energy Security Strategy (GGESS), established between Nigeria and the United States in 2005, marked an attempt to address the major issues affecting energy supplies in the region as a whole, including the lack of economic development and the problems of bunkering and money laundering. The GGESS was later expanded to include the United Kingdom, Canada, the Netherlands, Switzerland, Norway, and France, but it has been hampered by the unreliability of its local partner in Nigeria, the Nigerian National Petroleum Corporation (NNPC). The United States has given Nigeria tracking equipment in the hope of improving maritime security in the Gulf of Guinea and cracking down on the bunkering problem, but there is little to show for this initiative. The United Nations (UN) secretariat has said it is willing to set up a committee of experts to examine the problem of "blood oil"—the term used to describe the misery caused by oil bunkering—but is awaiting a formal request from Nigeria.

At the oil company level, a major international energy firm operating in Nigeria has said it will offer fingerprinting technology to the Nigerian government to help its efforts to trace stolen oil. The technique uses chemical analysis precise enough to identify the field from which the oil originated. It can even pick out small quantities of Nigerian oil that have been mixed in with oil from another source. There appears to be no good reason why the Nigerian government cannot use this technology to monitor the movement of blood oil.

Policy Recommendations

Finding a solution to the problem of armed groups in the Niger Delta requires coordinated action by the Nigerian government, the United States, and other international partners. Nigeria should

- *Clamp down on criminal activities, including bunkering, illegal arms importation, money laundering, and political thuggery.* This does not mean repeating the blunt military attacks of mid-May 2009, in which hundreds of innocent women, children, and elderly people were caught in the crossfire. Rather, the criminal activities that support and encourage militancy must be stopped. The militants must be denied an easy path back into crime. The government must not turn a blind eye to bunkering. It must pursue and prosecute members of the military who are involved in the illegal trade. Nigeria should accept offers of international help in tracking down the criminal networks, some of them led by foreign nationals, who direct bunkering operations. It should cooperate with international efforts to track down and apprehend vessels suspected of trafficking stolen oil, possibly accepting offers of assistance to improve maritime security. It should be more willing to share intelligence and work with nations where spot markets are based, encouraging them to play their part in cracking down on bunkering. In addition, there should be serious efforts made to go after the corrupt political figures who form and maintain armed groups for political violence.

The Situation in Rivers State

Rivers State's government is the wealthiest state government in Nigeria. That position is derived from Rivers' status as the heart of Nigeria's booming oil industry. Rising world oil prices in recent years have flooded Rivers State's treasury with a budget larger than those of many West African countries. In spite of this wealth, Rivers has some of the worst socioeconomic indicators in the world—its people lack access to employment, education, health care, and other basic needs. Instead of putting its massive oil revenues to work developing the state for the benefit of the entire population, Rivers' politicians have largely squandered the money through mismanagement and corruption. . . .

But Rivers' wealth has not just been squandered; it has also been put to work sponsoring violence and insecurity on behalf of ruling party politicians. Prior to the 2003 elections, then governor Peter Odili and his political associates lavishly funded criminal gangs that helped rig the election into a landslide victory for the ruling People's Democratic Party (PDP). Those gangs used the money at their disposal to procure sophisticated weapons. . . .

Over the years, gangs initially sponsored by Rivers' politicians have become involved in other forms of lucrative criminal activity. . . . In large part due to their political connections, these gangs have committed crimes with near-total impunity. The police have made no serious effort to press criminal charges against or apprehend any significant gang leader, even though several of them have lived openly in urban areas where their violent crimes resulted in murder and injury to ordinary Nigerians.

"Politics as War: The Human Rights Impact and Causes of Post-Election Violence in Rivers State, Nigeria," Human Rights Watch, March 2008.

- *Give the people of the Niger Delta more control over their resources.* Reforming Nigeria's Land Use Act, so that more money from oil production in the Niger Delta stays in the Delta, would remove one of the main grievances of the armed groups and the ordinary people who sympathize with them. However, this must be done in a way that guarantees that the money gets down to the people and is not siphoned off by corrupt politicians at the state and local government levels. Several recommendations have been made for directly giving residents of all communities affected by the oil industry a stake in the oil and gas production that affects their region so strongly. Residents would have a better reason to safeguard oil facilities if they had a greater sense of ownership of the industry. In addition, the federal government should keep its promise to improve the economic well-being of people in the Niger Delta and improve the woefully inadequate infrastructure of the region.

- *Reform the security services.* The military has too often been a hindrance rather than a help in the Niger Delta. The complaint of over-militarization in the Niger Delta is valid. Soldiers should be properly trained and paid and concerted efforts should be made to tackle corruption. Local youths could be used for pipeline surveillance, under the supervision of their communities.

- *Secure the borders* to stem the flow of illegal arms into the country. Special attention should be paid to Lagos port, where many of the weapons arrive.

- *Begin an effective disarmament, demobilization, and reintegration process for armed groups.* In return for handing in their weapons, militants should be offered real incentives to rejoin society and forsake their pasts— such as jobs, training, and the opportunity to earn a living. The government should set up a Niger Delta works program to provide jobs in construction and development projects for former members of armed groups. State governments should work with the major oil companies to offer training schemes for skilled jobs and contracting opportunities in the oil and gas industry. The demobilization process should be strictly followed, with a census taken of all militants, and their reintegration into society should be closely monitored. Under the terms of reintegration, an amnesty for past crimes will be necessary because it will be impossible to prosecute all those who have been involved in militant activity, including their military and political backers. The DDR process should be supervised by a neutral body, preferably the UN.

- *Offer counseling to militants to ease their transition back into society.* This would include help for individuals suffering from psychological trauma and drug addiction. Militants' families—many of whom will be reluctant to accept them back should also be offered help and support. Their communities will also need security assistance to prevent any flare-ups of violence as the reintegration process takes place.

- *Establish a compact with the people of the Niger Delta.* This would be very constructive in building a mutual commitment toward peace, security, and development between the government and the people of the Niger Delta.

The United States and other international partners should

- *Engage more with Nigeria.* The United States should press the Nigerian government to do more to address the problems of the Niger Delta by making it clear that it regards the situation as a concern for international security. The United States needs an official diplomatic presence in the Niger Delta, an area that is, after all, of growing strategic importance as a major energy supplier. By opening a consular office in the region, the United States would be able to monitor its problems more effectively and build alliances with civil society groups. The United States should consider appointing a special envoy to the Niger Delta.

- *Engage with bilateral and multilateral partners in a diplomatic push.* The United States should seek to build an international consensus on policies to help the Niger Delta. It should revive a revised and more effective Gulf of Guinea Energy Security Strategy and work closely with the UN, the World Bank, and other organizations engaged with Nigeria.

- *Help Nigeria tackle bunkering.* The United States should help Nigeria improve security along its coastline by helping to train a professional, well-equipped coast guard. It should offer technical assistance to trace stolen oil and tackle money laundering. It should name and shame identified sponsors of bunkering operations, place travel bans on offenders, and freeze any U.S. assets they may have.

- *Work with international companies operating in Nigeria to ensure that good corporate governance is practiced.* The suspicion remains among many in the Niger Delta that some oil companies have sponsored armed groups to intimidate host communities, and that by hiring teams to conduct pipeline surveillance, they may have unwittingly aided the formation of armed groups.

- *Promote good governance in Nigeria.* The United States should remind the government in Abuja that the situation in the Niger Delta will never improve while people do not trust their politicians or the security forces or have faith in the electoral process. The United States should urge Nigeria to make the fight against corruption its top priority.

- *Promote revenue transparency in Nigeria.* The United States should work with Nigeria in building institutions to monitor the movement of resources and the fair allocation of revenues. The Niger Delta will remain unstable as long as its people believe that their resources are being misallocated or stolen from them.

- *Be serious about development.* The United States should be helping to develop the major infrastructural projects and job training programs the Niger Delta needs, rather than the token projects currently undertaken. Assistance should come in the form of technical help, rather than money. The United States should offer support for civil society groups to monitor the performance of their elected officials.

Conclusion

The armed groups of the Niger Delta pose an immense challenge to policy makers. They have been a well-established feature of life in the region for decades, they feed off the wider community's genuine grievances, and their motives and objectives are wide-ranging and often in conflict. Furthermore, the focus of their anger—the oil industry—is virtually defenseless in the face of their attacks. With endless miles of undefended oil pipelines crisscrossing the Niger Delta, militants are able to commit acts of sabotage and oil theft at will. The sheer multitude of armed groups adds another layer of complexity. Identifying the groups and trying to decipher what they want is an immensely difficult task because of their nebulous structure and ever-shifting allegiances. Each group has a specific history and the picture varies greatly from state to state. While most are involved in criminal activities such as oil bunkering, arms dealing, and kidnapping, many also regard themselves as freedom fighters and have overtly political aims.

The situation on the ground changes by the day. January 2009 began with talk of a diplomatic breakthrough as two of the leading militants, Soboma and Ateke, spoke of their wish for a peace deal with the government. By the end of the month, the tone had drastically changed following a military attack on one of their camps in Rivers State. This was followed by the murders of the leaders of two major armed groups, apparently by one of the militants who had been calling for a peace deal. In May 2009, Ateke was once again calling for a peace agreement and amnesty to be overseen by a neutral international body. It appears that Tom Polo was also one of the inspirations behind the promise by the federal government of Nigeria to grant an amnesty for the militants. In early June 2009, the military carried out a number of fierce attacks on the camps of Tom Polo and other militant leaders in Delta and Rivers States. A government committee has also completed its recommendations for the amnesty promised to the militants by President Yar'Adua in April. It remains to be seen whether the militants accept the amnesty, and if so under what conditions, or if strikes against oil facilities accelerate.

Confronted by such a complicated, ever-changing picture, the Nigerian government has proved itself unable to fashion a coherent response. Not only has it failed to demobilize the armed groups, it has failed to address the range of socioeconomic grievances that lie behind their formation and continued appeal. It has done little to provide jobs, improve the infrastructure, clean up the environment, tackle corruption, or address security fears. Instead, a clique of politicians and military officials have sequestered the lion's share of the region's wealth and squandered it. Until the federal government begins dealing with these deep-seated problems, there seems little prospect of the armed groups laying down their weapons.

Yet insecurity in the Niger Delta is a problem not only for the Nigerian government. It is a problem for the United States and the wider world as well. It is in the United States' interest to improve its energy security and reduce the flow of arms, illicit oil, and illegal money transfers from Nigeria. A stable Niger Delta producing a steady supply of oil would also help to moderate world oil prices. It is therefore imperative that the United States and other international partners offer Nigeria all the help it needs to confront its armed groups. Because one thing is clear: allowing the problem to fester will be a recipe for further violence, instability, and energy insecurity.

> "It's too soon to assess the long-term effects of ten years of anarchic violence in the Niger Delta; the call for oil companies to leave indicates that the population has not been intimidated."

Oil Companies Should Be Expelled from the Niger Delta

Ebrima Sillah and Sam Olukoya

Ebrima Sillah and Sam Olukoya are journalists. In the following viewpoint, they report on the demand of Nigerian women's environmental rights activists that oil companies leave the Niger Delta. Activists note that oil companies have not only wreaked widespread and catastrophic environmental damage, but also have brought more violence against women in the form of increased rates of rape and sexual slavery. Activists argue that oil companies must leave or be expelled from the region and that contracts be renegotiated with ample participation from local community and activists groups to protect women and the environment.

As you read, consider the following questions:

1. When did the government offer a peace deal and amnesty to Niger Delta militants, according to the authors?

2. How many young men in the Niger Delta does the author say are receiving training in nonviolence and skill acquisitions?

3. According to Debbie Effiong, how would a greater participation of women in the political process in the Niger Delta affect the struggle for peace?

Nigerian environmental rights groups have been making the case for the expulsion of oil companies from the Niger Delta in the southeastern part of the country at the World Social Forum [WSF] in Dakar [Senegal, in 2011].

Speaking at a meeting organised by a group of Nigerian women's environmental rights activists, Goodison Jim Dorgu, the executive director of [an environmental] NGO [nongovernmental organisation] ... based in the oil-producing state of Bayelsa, said Nigerian civil society has come to the united conclusion that oil companies responsible for severe environmental degradation should leave without delay.

"We feel that the oil companies should leave the shores of the Niger Delta. There have to be fresh negotiations if there has to be oil extraction and communities should be at the dialogue to represent themselves in the negotiations," said Dorgu.

Violence Is a Key Concern

Dorgu was speaking at a Feb. 9 session at the World Social Forum in Dakar, organised by Nigerian environmental justice activists, mostly women from the oil-rich Niger Delta. Other speakers outlined how the oil industry has provoked violence in the delta, with women bearing the brunt of the assault.

Emem Okon, the head of the [Kebetkache] Women's Development and Resource Centre in the city of Port Harcourt, alleged that the oil companies' own security personnel have been involved in attacks on women. She also said the Nigerian army had committed grave violations of human rights.

"There are specific cases in Akwa Ibom State, where Shell brought in a Shell crew and they attacked women. A pregnant woman was shot dead. There are also cases in Ogoniland where the government set up the Rivers State Internal Security Task Force, and what these soldiers did was to use women as a weapon of war," said Okon.

"A lot of women were raped, a lot of young girls were taken into sexual slavery."

Sow the Wind, Reap the Whirlwind

The Nigerian army's operations in Ogoni peaked in the mid-1990s, in a brutal response to powerful mobilisation of people which had attracted international attention. Hundreds were killed and tens of thousands displaced; charismatic Ogoni leader Ken Saro-Wiwa and eight others were arrested and later executed by the government. The army carried out similar attacks elsewhere in the oil-rich southeast of the country.

The military campaign shattered nonviolent resistance, but gave rise to armed groups whose activities—a mixture of progressive demands and profiteering from kidnapping oil workers and the sale of stolen crude—badly disrupted the country's oil output.

Speaking to Terra Viva from her home in Port Harcourt, Debbie Effiong of the NGO Gender and Development Action, said environmental degradation, poverty, activism and violence are intertwined.

"The environment is part of the livelihood of women; the land sustains them as farmers. Their farmlands are destroyed through oil pollution. So the violence by the military to suppress the people's cause for environmental justice has prompted a lot of awareness among the women."

The Role of Armed Militants

She said that women are keen to take part in the struggle for environmental justice. But the growing role played by armed groups in the Niger Delta complicates matters.

"The violence by militants [the armed groups] affected women's participation in the struggle for environmental justice at the stage when criminality took over the activities of the militants. The criminal aspect of it did not favour the struggle of women. Some of them lost their husbands, some lost their children, and it affected them emotionally in their quest to continue the struggle."

The Nigerian government offered a peace deal and amnesty to delta militants in 2009; most groups accepted. Despite complaints that the government has not held up its end of the bargain—militants again carried out several attacks on oil installations at the end of 2010—nearly 27,000 young men are now undergoing skills acquisition courses and transformational training on nonviolence.

Activists Undaunted

It's too soon to assess the long-term effects of ten years of anarchic violence in the Niger Delta; the call for oil companies to leave indicates that the population has not been intimidated. Effiong says that women too are ready to reclaim a place in the region's political life.

"With an increase in the number of women aspiring for political positions—if women are given that chance in the coming elections, I believe there will be a major change positively in the way leadership is run in this country," she said. "If women are given the opportunity to occupy elected positions, it will definitely enhance the struggle."

In Dakar, Nnimmo Bassey, the head of Friends of the Earth International, told WSF participants that the struggle for environmental justice in the Niger Delta will be a long one.

"We are doing a lot of grassroots training and mobilisation and there are a lot of new groups coming up," said Bassey, who is himself from the Niger Delta.

"The regime of responsibility has been so well entrenched and there's the military backing for what the oil companies are doing, the government is behind them."

Bassey says there are many restrictions. "A lot more work is still going to be done, but one day, when nobody expects it . . . the people will prevail."

Periodical and Internet Sources Bibliography

The following articles have been selected to supplement the diverse views presented in this chapter.

Roger Bate	"Nigeria at 50," *Wall Street Journal*, October 7, 2010.
Nwaorgu Faustinus	"Niger/Delta: Militancy or Criminality a Genuine Case for Agitation?," Modern Ghana, January 27, 2011. www.modernghana.com.
Human Rights Watch	"Politics as War," March 26, 2008. www.hrw.org.
Bakare Najimdeen	"Violence in the Oil Basin: Why Niger Delta Violent Conflict Remains Violent," Nigerian-Newspaper.com, November 17, 2007. www.nigerian-newspaper.com.
Louis Odion	"Niger Delta 'Peace Process' as Circus," NGEX.com, January 21, 2008. www.ngex.com.
Victor Ojakorotu	"Militancy and Oil Violence in the Niger Delta," *Journal of Energy Security*, August 27, 2009.
Ike Okonta	"Nigeria's 2011 Elections Are Shaping Up to Be a Perfect Storm," *Daily Star*, October 29, 2010.
Bisi Olawunmi	"Nigeria's War Drums on Cote d'Ivoire," *Vanguard*, February 12, 2011.
Emmanuel Onwubiko	"Wanted—Goodluck Formula for Jos," *Leadership*, March 22, 2011.
Alex Thurston	"Recent Violence Prompting Questions About Niger Delta Strategy," *Christian Science Monitor*, October 27, 2010.

CHAPTER 3

How Serious Is the Corruption Problem in Nigeria?

Chapter Preface

On May 29, 2011, Goodluck Jonathan was sworn in as the fourteenth president of Nigeria. In his inaugural speech, he outlined the challenges ahead for his country. On that list—and one that is the most pressing in many people's eyes—was the problem of corruption. "The bane of corruption shall be met by the overwhelming force of our collective determination, to rid our nation of this scourge," Jonathan promised. "The fight against corruption is a war in which we must all enlist, so that the limited resources of this nation will be used for the growth of our commonwealth."

Despite attempts to stem the tide of corruption in Nigeria, it remains a persistent and major problem. In Transparency International's annual Corruption Perceptions Index (CPI), which measures the perceptions of corruption in relation to countries around the world, Nigeria is perceived to be one of the most corrupt places to do business. In a 2003 study, Nigerians asked to rank the most corrupt institutions pointed to the police, political parties, national and state assemblies, local and municipal governments, and federal and state executive councils as the worst offenders.

It is reported that corruption permeates every level of Nigerian society. Corrupt politicians get bribes from business leaders to pass laws advantageous to business. Corrupt policemen take kickbacks from organized crime syndicates to look the other way. Corrupt bureaucrats take bribes to do business or to not enforce regulations against certain individuals or businesses.

Although corruption is a universal problem, in Nigeria it is thought to be tolerated and accepted as a way of life. As Professor Ogaga Ifowodo observes on the Sahara Reporters site, "Corruption has become the oxygen Nigerian public office holders and their cronies breathe. Unchecked, it seems now our 'natural' way of life." Much of the blame for this passive and accepting attitude toward corruption is placed on Nigeria's history, particularly its colonial period under British rule. It was during this time, recent commentators claim, that Nigerians experienced a "colonial trauma" that doomed Nigeria to repeat the mistakes of the colonial era, during which British colonizers lived lavish lifestyles at the expense of impoverished and powerless Nigerians. As Nigerians coveted the easy and luxurious life of their British overlords, when it came their chance at self-rule they imitated the system of government they had become familiar with: corruption, graft, consumerism, and materialism as a sign of wealth and power.

Nigeria gained independence from England in 1960. In post-colonial Nigeria, corruption flourished under leaders that many historians view as corrupt, timid, or tolerant of institutionalized corruption. Accounts of many Nigerian leaders include tales of fixing elections, paying and receiving bribes, graft, charges of nepotism and favoritism, money laundering, arson, lapsed ethical judgment, and fraud.

As the reputation of Nigeria became associated with corruption and crooked government, there were also international and domestic forces working to address the problem. In 2003 Nigeria put in place the Economic and Financial Crimes Commission (EFCC), a law enforcement agency devoted to investigating and prosecuting financial crimes. The EFCC took on a number of high-profile corruption cases against government officials and business leaders, including the leaders of several banks.

In 2011 new strides were made in the fight against corruption in Nigeria. The election of Goodluck Jonathan signaled hope that Nigeria had elected a leader with the courage and fortitude to tackle the problem. In addition, Nigeria became the fifty-third country to sign the United Nations (UN) agreement on the International Anti-Corruption Academy (IACA), a UN body created to promote international cooperation and coordination in the fight against corruption. Although these steps do not fully address the scourge of corruption and crooked government that hinders Nigeria's economic and social development, they do mark a serious effort to finally confront and make progress on one of the country's most problematic issues.

The issue of corruption in Nigeria is the focus of the following chapter, in which topics include corruption in the media, the nature and scope of corruption in the country, and the importance of fair and transparent elections.

> "This legacy [of corruption] meant that by 2000 Nigeria was officially declared the world's most corrupt country by Transparency International."

There Is an Endemic Corruption Problem in Nigeria

Lanre Akinola

Lanre Akinola is a journalist and contributor to This Is Africa. *In the following viewpoint, he maintains that although Nigeria has made great progress in fighting corruption in the economic sector, it still has a long way to go. Key to that success is the continued efforts of the Economic and Financial Crimes Commission (EFCC), a government agency tasked with rooting out corruption, prosecuting criminals, and recovering public money. The problem of corruption, Akinola states, is institutionalized, and therefore, it will take a rigorous and systemized approach to eliminate.*

As you read, consider the following questions:

1. How much money does the author state was lost to mismanagement or theft between 1960 and 1999 in Nigeria?

2. According to the author, how much money was recovered by the EFCC from 2003–2008?

3. According to the 2009 Transparency International Corruption Perceptions Index, what does Nigeria rate?

O f all the factors that account for Nigeria's bumpy road since independence, few have the symbolic power of corruption. It is estimated that between 1960 and 1999 alone more than $440bn [billion] of public money was lost to mismanagement or theft, severely stifling institutional and economic development.

Successive military dictatorships since independence, notably that of Ibrahim Babangida from 1985 to 1993, are seen to have effectively institutionalised corruption. This legacy meant that by 2000 Nigeria was officially declared the world's most corrupt country by Transparency International.

"It is the root cause of our inability to really address all our issues," argues Nuhu Ribadu, the former executive chairman of Nigeria's Economic and Financial Crimes Commission, whose name has become a byword for anti-corruption activism in the country.

"When those who are entrusted with the responsibility to manage a country's resources for the common good end up using it selfishly, there is no way you can do anything ... sadly that has been the order in our own situation."

The Success of the EFCC

Mr Ribadu was instrumental in the establishment of the EFCC in 2003, which turned out to be a watershed moment in Nigerian history. Not a single public official had ever been success-

119

fully prosecuted on charges of corruption prior to then, and in the four years that he headed the agency, it sent shockwaves through Nigeria's political system. "We prosecuted our top-level people, including ministers, parliamentarians, and chief law officers. We recovered $5bn in a short amount of time and got almost 300 convictions," says Mr Ribadu.

The success of the EFCC made him and the agency household names, yet Mr Ribadu says that it could easily have been different.

"It was not planned, it was actually accidental. The EFCC itself was a creation of pressure from the outside world," he recalls.

A Pressing Need to Fight Corruption

In the wake of the September 11 [2001] terrorist attacks in the US, Nigeria found itself on the Financial Action Task Force's blacklist, containing countries considered to be major enablers of money laundering and potential terrorist financing. Removal required improvements to its anti–money laundering regime, part of which involved updating laws and establishing an agency to enforce them. It took officials two years to become aware of this list, at which point the new law was rushed through the legislature.

"Parliament did not take it seriously and nobody had any clue what they were signing. It was a piece of paper that was given to me. Nobody understood clearly what it was," Mr Ribadu explains. A reformist mood in the government allowed for this to turn into the agency that would later make such headlines. In [President] Olusegun Obasanjo "we had a leader who appreciated the fact that this was the right way to go. We also had a team of reformers getting into government," he says.

A Great Team

Notable amongst these individuals were the likes of Obiageli Ezekwesili and Ngozi Okonjo-Iweala, Mr Ribadu says. Ms

Ezekwesili is one of the founding members of Transparency International and served as a cabinet minister under Mr Obasanjo, while Ms Okonjo-Iweala served as minister of finance, and played a vital role in securing $18bn in debt relief for Nigeria in 2005. Both are now with the World Bank.

"We came together as a team and decided that we would try to create a government agency to demonstrate to people that something can be done. To some extent we succeeded in an almost impossible environment," Mr Ribadu says.

Controversy Emerges

The success of the EFCC has not been without controversy. Some have accused Mr Ribadu and the agency of aggressively pursuing political opponents of then president Olusegun Obasanjo while leaving him and his allies untouched. And while his actions as head of the EFCC gained him widespread popularity amongst ordinary Nigerians, it also earned him powerful enemies. Mr Ribadu found himself sidelined by incoming president Umaru Yar'Adua in 2007, and after surviving two assassination attempts he went into self-imposed exile in the USA.

"It was dangerous and risky, but it helped to change the psyche of people, causing them to look at things a bit differently and demonstrating that the possibilities are there," he says.

A Legacy of Anti-Corruption Efforts

While Mr Ribadu's days at the EFCC have come to an end, the agency is still running, and some have suggested that the actions of reformers over the past decade have paved the way for reform-minded Nigerians such as Lamido Sanusi, who was appointed governor of the central bank in 2009.

His public disclosure of widespread fraud amongst some of the country's major banks, and subsequent crackdown on

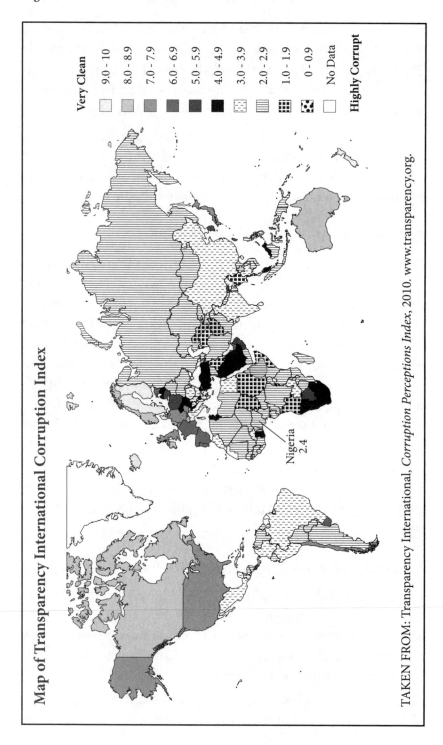

Map of Transparency International Corruption Index

TAKEN FROM: Transparency International, *Corruption Perceptions Index*, 2010. www.transparency.org.

top-level executives together with the EFCC made international headlines, resulting in a number of high-profile arrests and court cases.

A Long Way to Go

According to the 2009 Transparency International Corruption Perceptions Index, the country has improved significantly on its unenviable distinction in 2000, though with a score of 2.5 on the index—denoting that corruption is still perceived to be endemic—few are pretending that the struggle against corruption is anywhere near complete.

Ensuring that such efforts are sustained cuts to the very heart of the development challenges not just of Nigeria, but the continent as a whole, argues Mr Ribadu.

"If Africa is to have a chance to address its own problems we must go the direction we are going at the moment. We fought for independence, we fought to kick out the military—the last challenge is probably management and governance. And maybe if we get it right this time the whole process of development and growth will start taking place."

> *"While I accept that corruption is a se-*
> *rious issue, my personal opinion is that*
> *it is merely the symptom of a larger*
> *malaise."*

Corruption Is Not the Main Problem in Nigeria

Jideofor Adibe

Jideofor Adibe is a journalist and editor. In the following viewpoint, he argues that corruption is the result of much larger problems in Nigeria, particularly the issues of underdevelopment and weak institutions. It is not, as many people believe, a defining characteristic of the Nigerian people or the sign of moral weakness. Nigeria must fight the issues that give rise to social ills, attacking the problem at the root. Adibe also recommends a general amnesty program for corrupt politicians and individuals because Nigeria needs a clean slate when it comes to the issue of corruption.

As you read, consider the following questions:

1. What does Adibe identify as "a mortal political sin" that occurred in 1979?

Jideofar Adibe, "Is Corruption Really the Problem?," *Daily Trust*, February 17, 2011. Copyright © 2011 by *Media Trust Limited*. All rights reserved. Reproduced by permission.

2. Where was Nigeria ranked on the 2010 Transparency International corruption ratings?

3. How many paramilitaries linked to drug cartels were granted amnesty in Colombia in 2006?

Many commentators to my last week's piece [February 2011], 'Buhari's Bakare's Choice' disagreed with my contention that [Muhammadu] Buhari [a Nigerian politician who ran in the 2011 presidential election] appears to rely only on his charisma to win the election rather than develop a saleable programme. Most of those who wrote or sent text messages argued that Buhari's anti-corruption credentials are sufficient, and that once the cankerworm of corruption—the abuse of public office by officials—is tackled head-on, every other issue would fall in place. I respectfully disagree with this position but more on it later.

The flood of critical comments on the piece is perhaps an indication of the level of adulation Buhari enjoys, especially in the North. I have tremendous respect for the retired general's sense of patriotism and honesty. However, I also believe that as ordinary citizens we help our leaders to become better not by adoring them uncritically but by having the courage to critically interrogate their choices and policy options. To believe that our heroes can do no wrong is to imbue them with a messianic complex, which often leads to complacency and deterioration in their critical skills. We saw this vividly in 1979 when the highly revered [politician Obafemi] Awolowo committed a mortal political sin by choosing a fellow Christian and fellow southerner Chief Philip Umeadi as his running mate. Had Awolowo's strategists and admirers not been so starstruck or cowardly to question that choice, perhaps the outcome of the 1979 presidential election would have been different.

Corruption Is a Symptom

Now back to the argument that corruption is the bane of our society. I do not believe this. While I accept that corruption is a serious issue, my personal opinion is that it is merely the symptom of a larger malaise. It is wrong to elevate the institutional manifestation of a problem to its defining characteristic.

The belief that corruption is the bane of our society in fact raises other fundamental issues:

One, most Nigerian leaders generally see corruption as resulting from moral lapses on the part of the affected individuals rather than a symptom of a more fundamental systemic problem of underdevelopment, which interfaces with the crisis in our nation-building project and our weak institutions. This wrong diagnosis in turn seems to have led to the uncritical deification of people with the courage to go after 'big' corrupt men and women. If we have been right about corruption and the way to fight it, why has our ranking in the corruption perception index by Transparency International [an agency that measures corruption] continued to deteriorate despite the noise about EFCC [Economic and Financial Crimes Commission] and ICPC [Independent Corrupt Practices Commission]? For instance the list released by Transparency International on October 26, 2010, showed that we moved down from a ranking of 121 in 2008 to 130 in 2009 and to 134 in 2010. And by the way, what became of the previous contraptions and rhetoric used in fighting the ailment [corruption] such as Obasanjo's Jaji Declarations of the 1970s, Shagari's Ethical Revolution, Buhari-Idiagbon's War Against Indiscipline, Babangida's MAMSER and Abacha's dreaded Failed Bank Tribunals [all failed anti-corruption efforts].

Two, it will seem that the current strategies for fighting corruption exacerbate our underdevelopment crisis by undermining the growth of institutions while entrenching the fear of the 'strong ruler' who controls the contraptions used in the so-called fight against the social ill. In development circles, it is commonly believed that what Africa needs is strong institutions, not strong men. This means that credible leaders with the right vision and road map for addressing the problems that give rise to social ills like corruption will be more successful in the fight against the ailment than those whose credentials are based on fighting the symptom of a more fundamental problem. I am not by any means implying that Buhari is incapable of developing such a vision. In my opinion, Buhari is the most believable of all the presidential candidates in the field, meaning that had he developed a clear vision and road map, and based his candidacy on them, he would have broadened his support base. A good road map by the way is not just headline sound bites but must be able to tell us how an identified problem will be solved, the time line and milestones as well as where the money will come from.

Corrupt Investigations

Three, the fight against corruption in the country has historically been intertwined with political vendetta. For instance though both the Foster-Sutton Tribunal (1956) [an investigation that found Nnamdi Azikiwe, or Zik, guilty of ethical violations] and the Coker Commission (1962) [an investigation into questionable political funding practices] found Zik and Awolowo respectively guilty of corruption; everyone knew that politics intruded in their findings. Similarly could the federal government have withdrawn the charges against Nuhu Ribadu, including allegations that he sold confiscated properties to fictitious companies when he was EFCC chairman, if [President Umaru] Yar'Adua had remained the president? What role did vendetta play in Obasanjo's celebrated pursuit of the 'Abacha loot'?

Four, based on the above, it is time to consider a general amnesty programme for corrupt politicians and individuals

Cartoon by Arend Van Dam 12/16/10 "http://www.politicalcartoons.com./"

not only because the whole fight against the malaise has been distractive and grossly ineffective but also because the country desperately yearns for a new beginning and a new social contract. It is in fact a mistake to equate the humiliation of some politicians with progress in the fight against an ailment that is generalized in the society and manifests in different forms. Can anyone show how the monies allegedly recovered from corrupt individuals have impacted positively on the material circumstances of ordinary Nigerians? Can the recovered loots even be properly accounted for?

All over the world amnesty programmes are used to deal with problems that appear intractable or to offer a new beginning. In 2004 for instance, George W. Bush enacted a tax amnesty programme, which allowed US corporations to bring home, tax-free, the billions of dollars they stashed away in tax havens. In 2006, the government of Colombia granted amnesty to some 21,000 paramilitaries linked to drug cartels. In South Africa, the Truth and Reconciliation Commission offered amnesty to people who confessed and apologised for crimes committed under apartheid. Just before he became gravely ill and subsequently died, Yar'Adua also offered amnesty to militants of the Niger Delta in exchange for their laying down their guns. An amnesty programme will also encourage the repatriation of much-needed funds hidden in different parts of the world to help accelerate our economy.

The proposed amnesty should be one-off, and extend to other financial criminals such as drug barons and '419ers' because their crimes are no worse than the crimes of those who have benefited from amnesty here or in other countries. The amnesty should of course be predicated on certain conditions such as forfeiture of a certain percentage of the loot to the state which shall be managed as trust funds solely for employment generation and combating the problem of electricity. I sincerely believe that what the country urgently needs now is a new beginning and a leader who has the vision and road map to offer us such.

> "Democracy is more than a formal counting of votes, and both Nigerians and the international community will judge the quality of this election by more than what happens on Election Day."

Nigeria Must Have Fair and Transparent Elections

Terence P. McCulley

Terence P. McCulley is the US ambassador to Nigeria. In the following viewpoint, he emphasizes the importance of fair and transparent elections in Nigeria, stating that they are essential in the effort to fully establish the "institutions, practices, and values of democratic governance." He urges the Nigerian government to allow the registration of all eligible voters for the 2011 elections and not foment violence or acts of intimidation on Election Day. McCulley also reminds Nigerians, particularly the youth of the country, to vote and practice their civic duty.

As you read, consider the following questions:

1. What event did Nigeria celebrate in 2010?

2. According to the author, what recent challenges to democracy has Nigeria endured?

3. What does the author believe is Nigeria's most valuable and dynamic resource?

Last year [2010], Nigeria celebrated its golden jubilee. It was a signal event, marking 50 years of Nigerian independence, and celebrating Nigeria's emergence as a force on the world stage. This great nation has demonstrated its consequence throughout its history—supporting liberation movements on the continent, contributing to regional military actions in support of peace, security and humanitarian assistance, demonstrating economic capacity and entrepreneurial spirit, and engaging the world as a leader in the Economic Community of West African States (ECOWAS), the African Union, and at the United Nations.

The giant of West Africa has much of which to be proud. The time has now come for Nigeria to take the next step to achieve its potential by embracing democracy fully and cementing in place the institutions, practices, and values of democratic governance. Free, fair, and credible elections are an important part of that process.

Promoting democracy and respect for human rights has long served as the underpinning of American foreign policy, and President [Barack] Obama has underscored the importance of these first principles in our engagement abroad. We do not seek primacy for a specific democratic construct—democracy is as diverse as the global community—but we are convinced that advancing democracy has demonstrable dividends. Democratically governed nations deliver safer, more just, and more prosperous lives to their citizens. And strong democracies are more likely to secure peace, deter aggression, expand markets, promote development, combat terrorism and crime, uphold human rights and the rights of workers, avoid humanitarian crises, protect and improve the global environment, and protect human health.

America recognises that the pursuit of democracy is a difficult and organic process. Throughout our history, the United States has struggled to ensure that all citizens can fully enjoy the rights guaranteed under our laws and our Constitution. America's 39th president, Jimmy Carter, once stated: "The experience of democracy is like the experience of life itself—always changing, infinite in its variety, sometimes turbulent and all the more valuable for having been tested by adversity."

An Opportunity for Nigeria

Nigeria too has been tested by such adversity. Recently, Nigeria has endured term-limit challenges, the untimely death of a president, and the constitutional transfer of power to another. During its first 50 years, Nigeria survived a painful civil war and a pattern of military coups.

But enduring unexpected tests is not the same as addressing and correcting systemic or structural problems and the coming national elections present a golden opportunity for Nigeria to demonstrate its lasting commitment to democratic values and institutions.

Specifically, we urge political parties and the government to allow all registered voters to participate freely and fully in a peaceful and transparent process. This nation's political leadership—and all those who aspire to lead—must refrain from engaging in inflammatory rhetoric or supporting acts of intimidation. Violence has no place in a democratic society. We encourage efforts by the Nigerian government and civil society not only to permit, but to promote the inclusion of all political parties and their access to public fora and the media. Finally, whatever the outcome, we call on all political parties to respect the results of these elections.

Democracy is more than a formal counting of votes, and both Nigerians and the international community will judge the quality of this election by more than what happens on Election Day. Democracy is also about the freedom of all parties to campaign, meet with supporters, appeal to new voters, and deliver political messages to the electorate. Democracy is about sharing ideas and stimulating open public discussion on the future of one's country. Democracy is about upholding principles that are greater than any individual person and respecting the will of those who confer democratic legitimacy: the people of Nigeria.

Citizens Have Key Role

The Nigerian government is not solely responsible for the success of your elections. Representative and accountable government can only occur when citizens empower themselves by participating fully and actively in the democratic process, ensuring that their votes count. Only Nigerians, by their vote and their commitment to democracy, can ensure that the 2011 elections are truly free, fair and transparent.

Nigeria's most valuable and most dynamic resource is its people. Every day, whether meeting with entrepreneurs, government officials, civil society activists, farmers and shopkeepers, students and youth, I am impressed and inspired by the optimism, intelligence, drive, and ability of the Nigerian people. I am optimistic that the Nigerian people will decide what kind of government they want and then insist, even demand, that their leaders honestly represent their collective interests. Active citizen participation and open public involvement in all aspects of government is the most essential part of Nigeria's promising future.

And speaking about the future, I would like to offer a special message for the youth of Nigeria. You represent the majority in this country, and you all have individual decisions to make about where you want to be in the next five to ten years. But you have an equally important collective decision about where you want Nigeria to be in the next decade. Go out and vote. Choose wisely. Make your voices heard.

The challenge for Nigerians in the coming years will be to build solid institutions, based upon the legitimacy conferred by the country's strong, diverse and decent people, and guided by democratic principles. You can count on American support for this enterprise, because Nigeria matters in the sub-region, on the continent, and on the world stage. As you build and consolidate your democratic institutions, and with many friends and partners throughout the world, Nigeria will increasingly be called upon to lead in Africa and beyond. But it starts with you and your fellow citizens. And it starts now, in April, with these important elections.

> "One key recommendation . . . is to provide Nigerians with greater information about the resources and responsibilities of their local representatives so that the public can hold leaders accountable."

Nigerians Must Demand More Accountability from Their Officials

Olumide Taiwo and Nelipher Moyo

Olumide Taiwo is an Africa research fellow and Nelipher Moyo is a research analyst at the Brookings Institution. In the following viewpoint, they maintain that Nigerian governmental officials are not accountable to the people and have allowed corruption to run wild. They also argue that improvements to transparency and accountability are the cure to the endemic problem of corruption. A commitment of the Nigerian people to work toward these things is essential to moving Nigeria forward and reaching its full political, economic, and social potential.

Olumide Taiwo and Nelipher Moyo, "Reforms to Improve Local Accountability in Nigeria," Brookings Institution, September 6, 2011. www.brookings.edu. Copyright © 2011 by the Brookings Institution. All rights reserved. Reproduced by permission.

As you read, consider the following questions:

1. What, according to the authors, has Nigeria's president, Goodluck Jonathan, placed at the forefront of his political agenda?

2. According to the authors, why is Nigeria's existing framework particularly vulnerable to abuse?

3. What solutions do the authors recommend to improve accountability?

Nigeria's president, Goodluck Jonathan, appears to have placed good governance at the forefront of his political agenda. He is considering a constitutional amendment that would limit governors and presidents to a single longer term in office. This proposal is aimed at reducing the violence and political jockeying associated with elections in Nigeria by ensuring a candidate only stands for one election with a longer "breathing space" between elections. President Jonathan is said to be considering an additional set of reforms, the most effective of which is to do away with the state-local council joint accounts and to grant Nigeria's 774 local governments financial autonomy. Local councils in Nigeria represent the third layer of government after the federal government and state governments. Federal and state government allocations to local councils are deposited into special "state joint local government accounts." Through these accounts, local governments are supposed to finance primary, adult and vocational education, agriculture and natural resource development, as well as health services.

Vulnerability to Abuse

Unfortunately, the existing joint account framework has been particularly vulnerable to abuse. Local council chairmen are typically nominated by political party "kingmakers" who help to finance their election campaigns. Because politicking in the country is quite expensive, federal allocations to local councils have become the means of paying back "kingmakers" for supporting their election campaigns. Keeping the political party happy is often at the forefront of councilmen's agendas and addressing the needs of the local constituents—who have very little say in who stands for election—comes second. By the time the political party elites receive their share of the funds and the council chairmen remove their "entitlement," there is very little left for local council development programs. Local council leaders are beholden to the entrenched interests of their political parties and those who refuse to "share" federal government allocations are often not nominated for re-election. Some devastating consequences of this misuse are demonstrated in the country's high infant mortality and low literacy rates: Nigeria is ranked among the top 10 countries with the highest infant mortality rate in the world (91.54 deaths/1,000 live births) and it has an adult literacy rate of only 61 percent. These outcomes are likely to improve if local governments are given greater financial autonomy.

Granting local government's financial autonomy is necessary to facilitate local development by creating the space for local leaders to invest in their constituents and to limit the opportunities for abuse by political parties. Critics of the proposal to eliminate state-local council joint accounts point to a few instances of success as justification for maintaining the status quo. The most commonly cited "success" case is in Lagos State, where Governor Babatunde Fashola has facilitated significant local development by managing resources prudently. However, Mr. Fashola particularly stands out because he is an anomaly; very few governors have managed their state's resources as prudently as Mr. Fashola. Local development should not only be possible when "accidental altruists" become state governors because, frankly, such leaders are rare.

The History of Nigeria's War on Corruption

Every community in Nigeria has mechanisms for dealing with corruption.... The fight in the public sector came to the limelight in 1966 when the military gave the reason of corruption of the politicians as one of the reasons for taking over. Experience later showed that the military is probably more corrupt than civilian politicians. The military ruled Nigeria from 1966–1979 and handed over power to the Alhaji Shehu Shagari administration in 1979. But barely four years later, the Shagari administration was overthrown by the Buhari/Idiagbon regime [referring to the administration of President Muhammadu Buhari and his chief of staff Tunde Idiagbon]. The Buhari/Idiagbon regime launched a war against corruption, tried and jailed many politicians and dismissed many civil servants. But when the IBB [Ibrahim Babangida] regime overthrew the Buhari regime, it released many of the politicians that were jailed by the Buhari regime and reduced the sentences of others. In fact, it has been argued that "Babangida's government was unique in its unconcern about corruption within its ranks and among public servants generally; it was as if the Government existed so that corruption might thrive." There is no doubt that scholars are in agreement that corruption reached unprecedented levels in incidence and magnitude during the General Ibrahim Babangida regime.... By the time President Olusegun Obasanjo came back to power as a civilian president in 1999, corruption had reached unprecedented proportion that it formed a major portion of his inaugural speech.

Otive Igbuzor, "Youth and the War Against Corruption in Africa: Roles and Policy Options," presented at the National Youth Summit on Corruption and Corrupt Practices in Nigeria, September 9, 2005.

Increasing Accountability

The World Bank's Quantitative Service Delivery Survey (QSDS) of Nigeria's health care sector found evidence of widespread leakage in public resources in the delivery of primary health services by local governments. In one state, 42 percent of health staff had not been paid for 6 months due to public resource leakages. One key recommendation from that study is to provide Nigerians with greater information about the resources and responsibilities of their local representatives so that the public can hold leaders accountable.

There is a valid concern that financial autonomy for local governments will not necessarily reduce theft or mismanagement. Evidence suggests that councilmen's fortunes change dramatically within months of assuming office in ways that their salaries and allowances cannot support. Nigeria needs strong institutions that impose constraints on leaders so that outcomes are not dependent on the characteristics of leaders, but rather on the institutions themselves. In order to institute good governance in the country, President Jonathan must find ways to ensure council financial autonomy is accompanied by credible instruments that make the council chairmen answerable to local constituents.

Historically, one of the most common accountability mechanisms was for people to "vote with their feet" in protest of poor or corrupt leadership. Constituents would simply move elsewhere to escape bad leadership. This is not realistic in modern states with fixed borders. In advanced democracies, local councils have functioned well because of effective checks that balance political party objectives and local constituency interests. However, these checks are weak or nonexistent in Nigeria. Elsewhere in West Africa and particularly in Ghana, political parties are, by law, not involved in local elections. Local constituents vote for candidates not based on party affiliation but on visible credentials. Barring political parties from participation in local government elections would remove the stronghold political parties have on local councilmen. While a plan to adopt this system is unlikely to receive high-level support, it is certainly worth consideration.

Additional Recommendations

In addition to providing more information about local government budget allocation and use, we recommend the Nigerian constitution be amended to allow the people to recall nonperforming elected local government officials. It is not enough to simply provide more information to the public, there needs to be mechanisms for citizens to act on that information. The power to recall officials will ensure elected officials prioritize the needs of their local constituents and deliver promised goods and services.

Ultimately, average Nigerians do not care about how long the president or governor is in office, they care about a system that can effectively deliver the necessary goods and services needed for their well-being. Strategies to improve governance in Nigeria should be centered on how to design a system that is more accountable to people at this level.

Periodical and Internet Sources Bibliography

The following articles have been selected to supplement the diverse views presented in this chapter.

Sam Adesua	"Founded Fears," *Nigerian Tribune*, January 11, 2011.
Gabriel Akinadewo	"Judiciary for Sale," *Nigerian Compass*, August 13, 2011.
Peter Akpochafo	"Is Corruption Really the Problem?," *Nigerian Pilot*, February 25, 2011.
Daily Champion	"Freedom of Information Bill—Not Yet Uhuru," March 23, 2011.
Human Rights Watch	"Nigeria: Corruption and Misuse Rob Nigerians of Rights," January 31, 2007. www.hrw.org.
Ignatius Kaigama	"Nigeria at 50: Tackling Corruption and Poverty," *Guardian* (UK), October 1, 2010.
Barack Murtala	"Where Is My Freedom of Information Bill?," *Daily Independent*, May 24, 2011.
Christopher Odetunde	"Nigeria's Corruption Problems Need Citizen-Oriented Solutions," Nigeriaworld.com, July 12, 2007. http://nigeriaworld.com.
Hamilton Odunze	"Should Corruption Be Institutionalized in Nigeria?," African Analyst, April 13, 2011. www.africananalyst.net.
Alex Perry	"A Failure of Democracy in Nigeria," *Time*, April 23, 2007.
Tom Zeller Jr.	"Is Nigeria's Anti-Corruption Commission Corrupt?," *New York Times*, February 7, 2007.

OPPOSING
VIEWPOINTS®
SERIES

CHAPTER 4

What Challenges Does Nigeria Face?

Chapter Preface

On November 17, 2010, Nigerian president Goodluck Jonathan spoke at a meeting with international leaders from politics and finance and promised that his country would finally solve its major power supply problem. Despite massive investments and planned improvements to the power infrastructure in the country, Nigeria still suffers frequent power outages and blackouts. In some parts of the country, citizens go without power for weeks. Critical institutions and businesses, such as hospitals and factories, have to rely on noisy and pollution-spewing generators to ensure a stable power supply. For a country looking to grow and appeal to international businesses and development, the lack of a reliable power supply is a critical problem. It has been such a persistent stumbling block in the country's development that Jonathan has pegged it as one of his top priorities.

Energy experts state that Nigeria currently needs between 6,000 to 10,000 megawatts to achieve a fairly stable power supply; however, the current output is estimated by the government at 4,000 megawatts. During the 2010 meeting with international leaders, Jonathan projected that domestic power generations would rise to approximately 20,000 megawatts by 2015—enough to provide a stable supply of power for the needs of larger manufacturing industries as well as new industries and businesses that Nigeria is looking to attract and develop in the next few years. By April 2011 homes, offices, and commercial businesses would have a stable supply of electricity, he also predicted. This would be accomplished by the completion of a new national power transmission super grid with enough capacity to provide a growing Nigeria with all the power it would need to become a true economic and manufacturing powerhouse in Africa. In 2010 Jonathan approved $3.5 billion to build the super grid.

Jonathan also proposed privatizing much of the power industry. This would involve breaking up the government-run monopoly into generation, transmission, and distribution companies and then selling them off to the private sector. The hope would be that private industries would assume the cost and be more efficient, productive, and innovative in their approach to providing power to all Nigerians.

During a speech in July 2011, Jonathan addressed the power supply issue, acknowledging its importance to Nigeria's growth and development. "Our idea is to transform the economy to create space for all of us to operate," he said. "We are emphasizing on the power sector. Power has been one of our key points in our process of transforming the country. We are saying that in the next four years, for God's sake, Nigerians should have stable power so that small and medium scale enterprises can thrive. Our focus is to support the small and medium scale enterprise that employs more than 70 percent of our people to be very vibrant, and we cannot do it without power."

Critics, however, have been skeptical of Jonathan's predictions. He certainly wasn't the first to promise massive improvements to the power supply. Earlier administrations had promised the same thing and had failed miserably. Over the last decade, the Nigerian government has spent more than $16 billion dollars on building six new power stations and repairing transmission grids. The new stations, however, have been plagued by construction delays and cost overruns. Some critics charged that corruption and a lack of political will—two issues that seem to consistently plague Nigeria's political and economic sectors—crippled important upgrade and repair projects.

Jonathan's proposal to privatize the industry has also come under attack. Critics argue that private industry is rife with corruption and mismanagement and that important public services, such as power generation, should not be entrusted to private businesses that care only about the bottom line. Instead of lowering the price of electricity, private industries will work to raise the price to generate greater profit—all at the expense of the public good.

The issue of a stable power supply is one of the issues explored in the following chapter, which outlines some of the key challenges Nigeria faces in the near future. Other viewpoints discuss the safety of Nigerian airports, the government's commitment to women's rights, and the debate of the same-sex marriage prohibition act.

> *"Despite the provisions of the protocol [on the rights of women in Africa] recognising and guaranteeing rights and the obligation of the Nigeria government, the lives of Nigerian women [have] yet to attain a commensurate level of improvement."*

Nigeria Must Fulfill Its Commitment to Protect Women's Rights

Omoyemen Odigie-Emmanuel

Omoyemen Odigie-Emmanuel is a Nigerian lawyer, researcher, and gender advocate and one of the founders of the Centre for Human Rights. In the following viewpoint, she maintains that despite the adoption of the protocol on the rights of women in Africa by the full African Union, Nigeria has failed to show a commitment to the principles of the document. Odigie-Emmanuel asserts that the Nigerian government has the obligation to pass relevant laws to support the goals of the protocol and allocate funds to women's rights issues and organizations. Doing so will go a long way in redeeming the government's tarnished image on the women's rights issue.

As you read, consider the following questions:

1. When was the protocol on the rights of women in Africa adopted by the African Union?

2. What legislation does the author feel the Nigerian National Assembly needs to pass to prove its commitment to women's rights?

3. What three forms of marriage are recognized in Nigeria, according to the author?

The Protocol to the African Charter on Human and Peoples' Rights on the Rights of Women in Africa is a unique piece of legislation because it takes into consideration the provisions of other international instruments on human rights that touch on women's rights, the need for equality and freedom from discrimination. It also takes into consideration the peculiar circumstances of women in Africa and their vital role in development. The protocol certainly could have been the key to a new dawn for Nigerian women, but the sad thing is that the reality seems a far cry away. You can only stare and wonder if some hearts thought before they signed.

This [viewpoint] seeks to appraise the unique provisions contained in the protocol, assess the current situation of women in Nigeria and ask, 'How far has the protocol helped the situation of women's rights in Nigeria? What needs to be strengthened and what are the glaring gaps in implementation?'

The Protocol

The protocol was adopted on 11 July 2003 by the AU [African Union] to strengthen the promotion and protection of women's rights. The preamble highlights several considerations necessitating the protocol. These considerations include a recognition of Article 2 of the African Charter on Human and Peoples' Rights, which enshrines the principle of nondiscrimination. It includes Article 18, which calls on all states to eliminate discrimination against women. It also includes provisions which recognise women's essential role in development, the principle of promoting gender equality as enshrined in the Consultative Act of the AU as well as the New Partnership for Africa's Development. The considerations also take into account other relevant declarations, resolutions and decisions which underline the commitment of African states to ensure the full participation of African women as equal partners in Africa's development.

By virtue of the protocol, Nigerian women are guaranteed the right to dignity; the right to life, integrity and security of persons; freedom from harmful practices which negatively affect the human rights of women; equal rights in marriage; equal rights in cases of separation, divorce and annulment; the right to equal protection and benefit of the law; the right to participate in political and decision-making processes; the right to a peaceful existence and participation in the promotion and maintenance of peace; the right to education and training; equal opportunity in work and career advancement; the right to health, including sexual and reproductive rights; the right to food security; the right to adequate housing; the right to a positive cultural context; the right to a healthy and sustainable environment; the right to sustainable development; widow's rights; the right to equitable share in inheritance; the right of elderly women to special protection and freedom from violence; the right of women with disabilities to special protection and freedom from violence; the right of women in distress to special protection; and a right of remedy to any woman whose right or freedom has been violated.

The Obligations of the Nigeran Government

The obligation of the Nigerian government under the protocol includes ensuring that women enjoy the rights mentioned above through the following actions:

1. Enactment of appropriate legislation to combat all forms of discrimination, and specifically to prohibit all forms of violence against women; to ensure prevention, punishment and eradication of violence against women; to prohibit and punish all forms of genital mutilation; to guarantee that no marriage takes place without free will and between consenting adults; to ensure that men and women have the same right during separation, divorce and annulment of marriage; and to guarantee equal opportunity in work and career advancement.

2. Appropriate and effective education, administration, prohibition, protection, promotion, institutional, implementation and regulatory measures.

3. Integrating a gender perspective in policy decision.

4. Modifying social and cultural patterns of conduct of women and men through public education, information and communication.

5. Positive action to promote participation of women in politics and decision making.

6. Provision of effective remedies.

7. Ensuring full implementation at the national level.

8. Providing budgetary and other resources necessary for full and effective implementation.

So far, some of the positive actions taken by the Nigerian government are:

- Adoption of a gender policy in 2007;

- Establishment of science schools for girls;

- Establishment of women development centres in 36 states;

- Adoption of the Trafficking in Persons (Prohibition) Law Enforcement and Administration Act;

- Establishment of a national agency for the prohibition of trafficking in persons;

- Adoption of a national policy on HIV/AIDS, reproductive health and female genital mutilation.

Aspects hindering the rights of women include:

- The patriarchal structure of Nigerian society;

- Failure of the National Assembly to pass the Abolition of All Forms of Discrimination Against Women In Nigeria and Other Related Matters Bill and failure to pass a national bill prohibiting violence against women.

- Failure of the government to domesticate the protocol or enact appropriate legislation necessary for bringing to pass its obligations and undertakings under the protocol is worrying.

The questions that come to mind are: Why did the Nigerian government sign the protocol? Did the government sign as a mere formality, knowing that the protocol could be frustrated by non-domestication by virtue of Section 12 of the Constitution? Or is there just a divorce between the arm of government that signs international instrument and the arm that domesticates these agreements? Or do we align our thinking with Richard Falk, who says: 'For various reasons associated with public opinion and prides, governments are quite ready to endorse (even formerly) standards of human rights despite their unwillingness to uphold these standards in practice.'

The Nigerian Reality

Despite the provisions of the protocol recognising and guaranteeing rights and the obligation of the Nigeria government, the lives of Nigerian women [have] yet to attain a commensurate level of improvement. Women rank lower than men in all indices of development in the country.

Economic and Social Welfare Rights

Paul Ogunyomi [an expert writing for the Department of Industrial Relations and Personnel Management at the University of Lagos], writing on the typologies of discriminative practices in the Nigerian workplace, identified sex discrimination as being prevalent in Nigeria. This takes the form of a woman being treated less favourably than a man on the grounds of sex, or indirectly by conditions applied equally to men and women which are detrimental to women.

Research reveals that adequate maternity leave is important to enable the woman's body to recover after delivery. A study of the Nigerian workplace has revealed that '... gap is identified between law and practice with wide patterns of protection resulting in some women enjoying good benefits, while others are wholly or partly unprotected within the Nigeria workplace....'

Women still have a higher unemployment rate than men. Those employed are concentrated in the informal sectors like agriculture, petty trading and services. Homemaking is still not recognised or compensated.

Health and Reproductive Rights

With a maternal mortality ratio of 704 to 1,000 per 100,000 live births, Nigeria continues to have one of the highest levels of maternal mortality. Incidences of gender-based violence have health consequences and result in health complications including miscarriages, long-term disabilities, unwanted pregnancies, HIV/AIDS and other sexually transmitted diseases.

The Practice of Female Genital Mutilation in Nigeria

The practice of female genital mutilation (FGM) is widespread covering practically every state of the federation [of Nigeria], though in varying magnitude from infancy to adulthood. Some sociocultural determinants have been identified as supporting this avoidable practice. It has not been possible to determine when or where the tradition of FGM originated. It is still deeply entrenched in the Nigerian society, where critical decision makers are grandmothers, mothers, women, opinion leaders, men and age groups. The reasons given to justify FGM are numerous; they include custom and tradition; purification; family honour; hygiene; aesthetic reasons and protection of virginity and prevention of promiscuity. Others include increased sexual pleasure of husband; enhancing fertility; giving a sense of belonging to a group and increasing matrimonial opportunities.

"Elimination of Female Genital Circumcision in Nigeria,"
World Health Organization, December 2007.

Right to Education and Training

Access to education is still low, especially in the northern parts of the country where withdrawal of girls for the purposes of marriage or for caregiving is still practiced. According to ActionAid [International], '. . . educational developments in northern Nigeria is lagging behind other parts of the country on practically every indicator, number of facilities, transition rates, girls' enrolment, number of teachers. . . . The girls are hawking wares or doing household chores. . . . Low girls' enrolment is bound to aggravate gender imbalances that skew present and future opportunities against women.' Nationwide, gender gaps still exist at the higher levels of education.

Right to Participation in Political and Decision-Making Processes

Significant advances have been made in the area of women's participation in governance, yet the political participation of women in Nigeria remains one of the lowest in the world. Women's participation in government is still below the 35 per cent stipulated in the gender policy.

Marriage, Separation, Divorce and Women's Property Rights

Although Article 7 of the protocol provides for both parties of a marriage to enjoy equal rights within and after the marriage, in issues of custody and access to an equitable share of the joint property deriving from the marriage, this is not the case. Three forms of marriages are recognized in Nigeria—customary, Islamic and legislative marriage. The reality of women married under customary and Islamic law has not yet been affected by the protocol. A woman married under customary law is entitled to be provided with a home by her husband as long as the marriage lasts. She is also entitled to use her husband's property, but cannot dispose of it as her own. The right to be provided with a house by her husband terminates upon divorce. Upon divorce, a woman married under customary law has no claim over a house jointly owned by her husband. Her position is not helped by the provisions of the Matrimonial Causes Act in respect of maintenance and settlement of property, which expressly excludes the application of its provisions to marriages under customary and Islamic law. However, in the case of women married under law, where she is able to produce documents showing she made a contribution to the property, she is entitled to the part of the property commensurate to her contribution. Many women are denied custody and access to their children. Among those under Islamic law, child marriage is still prevalent. According to BAOBAB for Women's Human Rights, '. . . girls are often married between the ages of 9–14. The occurrence of child marriage is common.'

Violence Against Women

The protocol guarantees women freedom from violence. In reality, there is a prevalence of violence against women in our society. Violence takes several forms, including domestic violence, early and forced marriages, female genital mutilation, widow torture and inheritance-related violence. There are also direct forms of violence against women in Nigeria. For instance, in discussing the impact of the activities of militias, cults and security forces on women in the Niger Delta, Emem Okon states, '. . . When a culture of armed gang violence takes root in a society that does not recognise and respect women's rights, the result is a higher level of gender-based violence against women. In this case, the proliferation of guns in the Niger Delta has increased the risk that girls and women will be targets of sexual assault.' In another section of the same article, she stated that, 'The consequence has been disastrous, as women have suffered massive massacre, rape, sexual abuse, social psychological trauma . . . aggravated poverty, unemployment, hunger, anger, low self-esteem, bitterness, frustration, desperation, fear, tension and more conflicts.'

Some violence is performed by law enforcement agents. This can be direct or indirect. Direct assault by security officers is becoming prevalent. For instance, a case was brought before the Gwagwalada High Court in Abuja in which a policeman raped two girls. In the Odioma community of Brass Local Government in the Niger Delta, Amnesty International reported a case where a rape victim described how she was raped alongside her mother by security officers. Two months pregnant at the time, she lost her baby.

Access to Justice and Equal Protection Under the Law

The Constitution and certain laws in Nigeria still contain discriminatory aspects. For instance, Section 26(2) of the Constitution does not allow a Nigerian woman to transmit her nationality to her husband if he is a foreigner. Section 55[46] of the Penal Code applicable in northern Nigeria permits wife battery as chastisement, as long as grievous harm is not afflicted. Section 55 of the Labour Act prohibits women from working in the night.

Elimination of Harmful Practices, Culture and Discrimination Against Women

In some parts of Nigeria, women are still regarded as part of the husband's property and as such she cannot inherit her husband's property, but must be inherited alongside his other property by another male of the family. Also 'a lot of customs still continue unabated . . . that infringe greatly on the human rights of women.'

According to the National Human Rights Commission (NHRC), challenges to the promotion and protection of women's rights still include harmful tradition practices such as female genital mutilation, widowhood rites, child marriage and violence against women.

Right to Inheritance

In most parts of Nigeria, female children are still discriminated against on issues of inheritance. With the decision in *Mojekwu v. Mojekwu*, in which the Court of Appeal declared the 'oli-ekpe' custom of Nnewi—which permits the son or the brother of a deceased person to inherit his property to the exclusion of his female children—discriminatory, it was expected that discrimination against women and the girl child on the issue of inheritance would end. This is definitely not the reality, probably because the decision has not gained nationwide popularity and poverty prevents women from going to court to assert their rights.

Poverty and the Right to Dignity, Food Security and Adequate Housing

One major hindrance to the right to dignity, food security and adequate housing in Nigeria is poverty. Although Nigeria is richly endowed with both human and material resources, the Nigerian government, Nigerian civil society and the UNDP [United Nations Development Programme] all state that approximately 70 per cent of Nigerians are poor. The majority of the poor are women. Also, Nigeria does not have a social security plan for providing food and housing to the poor. This makes the situation of women precarious and exposes them to the sex trade and destitution.

The Right to a Healthy Environment and Sustainable Development

Every woman in Nigeria has a right to a healthy environment that is favourable to their development. In reality, the environment in Nigeria has not been favourable to the development of women.

According to [researchers] Abiola and Iyare, 'Since oil struck four decades ago, the ecological and environmental hazards from indiscriminate exploration have constituted an affront on the community and the survival of its people . . . the effects of oil exploration has produced debilitating effects on the peoples' traditional occupation—fishing and farming. . . .'

When the environment is degraded, as is the current situation in Nigeria, women are most affected because of their culturally and socially defined roles and responsibilities, because their adaptive capacity is low due to poverty and because their livelihoods are tied to the environment. In sum, any damage to the environment is damage to women as it affects their potential and their productivity.

Recommendations

The rich provisions of the protocol recognising and guaranteeing women's human rights in Nigeria promises a beautiful future for women—if the government fulfills its obligations.

In light of the current realities, government should redeem its image and show its commitment by:

- Domesticating the protocol;

- Passing the bill on violence against women;

- Reviewing laws on women's property rights and all other laws discriminating against women;

- Adequate budgetary allocations to issues that promote women's rights and bridge gender gaps;

- Integrating women's rights issues and gender education into the school curriculum.

> "What children learn, retain and practice after leaving school has direct impact on the nation's competencies and skills."

Nigeria Must Improve Its Schools

V.O. Ochuba

V.O. Ochuba is a writer for Education, *a professional journal presenting studies and theoretical papers on all areas of teaching and learning. In the following viewpoint, Ochuba asserts that Nigeria has a long way to go when it comes to creating twenty-first-century schools that produce students who will excel in today's rapidly changing world. Ochuba insists that quality education must be well organized and coordinated to be effective. Ochuba also maintains that problems with Nigeria's school inspectors, and the inspection process in general, have contributed to the low quality of education in Nigeria. The author outlines recommendations for improving education in Nigeria, such as ample government funding and adequate training for school inspectors.*

As you read, consider the following questions:

1. According to Ochuba, what is the federal inspectorate service of the Federal Ministry of Education directly responsible for in Nigeria?

2. What is the role of an education inspector in Nigeria?

3. Why, according to the author, is school inspection so important in Nigeria?

It is a known fact that education is the instrument for economic empowerment and development of sustainable economy. No wonder, one of the national education goals is "the acquisition of appropriate skills and the development of mental, physical and social abilities and competencies as equipment for the individual to live and contribute to the development of the society". [R.] Nwangwu (2007) opined that what children learn, retain and practice after leaving school has direct impact on the nation's competencies and skills. What is learnt both formally and informally thus determines the individual's ability to contribute to national development. According to [J.A.] Aghenta (2006), trained or educated human resources constitute manpower and personnel that bring about national development. It therefore means that the quality of education received by the citizens determines the level of development of any nation.

The Decline in Quality of Nigeria's Schools

There has been a public outcry on the continual decline in the standards of education in the country especially as indicated in public examination and the performance of education outputs that are inadequate for employment. For instance, FME [Federal Ministry of Education] (2006) reported that an average of 13.8 percent and 20.72 percent of candidates who sat for the West African Senior School Certificate Examination (WASSCE) and the National Examinations Council (NECO) between 2000 and 2006 had five credits (including mathematics and English) respectively. Employers of labour also complain about low performance of graduates from the nation's institutions of higher learning.

A number of factors determine the level of performance in the school system especially the quality of the input and school process variables. [V.O.] Ochuba (2008) opined that goals of education can only be achieved with a well-organized school system that would ensure that all aspects of school life are well articulated and effectively coordinated. For the education industry to carry out its functions of developing quality human capital, there is need for checks and balances by regular and effective supervision and inspection. [B.] Wilcox (2000) defined inspection as the process of assessing the quality and/or performance of institutions, services, programmes and projects by those (inspectors) who are not directly involved in them and who are usually specially appointed to fulfill these responsibilities. The federal inspectorate service of the Federal Ministry of Education is directly responsible for quality control and maintenance of standards in institutions below the tertiary level.

Unfortunately, the inspectorate services both at the state and federal levels have not lived up to expectation. This is because the inspectorate service is plagued by a number of issues and challenges. A study carried out by [M.A.] Ogunu (2001) revealed that inadequate numbers of inspectors, inadequate funds for inspection, lack of transportation among others were some of the problems encountered by inspectors. He also noted that 88% of the respondents reported that inadequate numbers of inspectors was a serious constraint to school inspection. Compounding the problems of inadequate numbers of inspectors is the low quality of personnel recruited into the inspectorate. Ogunu's study aforementioned shows that only 15 inspectors in Edo State inspectorate department are to visit 1008 primary and 145 secondary schools

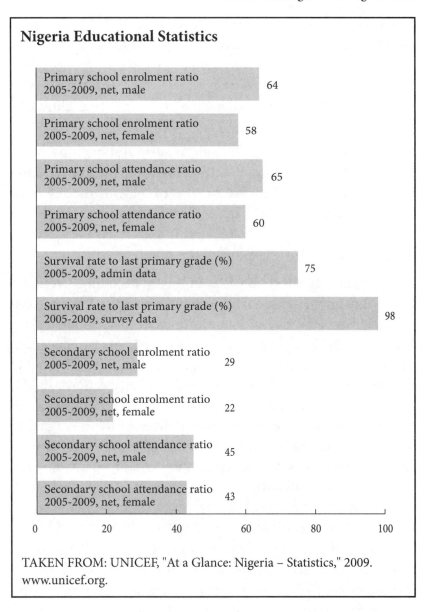

Nigeria Educational Statistics

Primary school enrolment ratio 2005-2009, net, male	64
Primary school enrolment ratio 2005-2009, net, female	58
Primary school attendance ratio 2005-2009, net, male	65
Primary school attendance ratio 2005-2009, net, female	60
Survival rate to last primary grade (%) 2005-2009, admin data	75
Survival rate to last primary grade (%) 2005-2009, survey data	98
Secondary school enrolment ratio 2005-2009, net, male	29
Secondary school enrolment ratio 2005-2009, net, female	22
Secondary school attendance ratio 2005-2009, net, male	45
Secondary school attendance ratio 2005-2009, net, female	43

TAKEN FROM: UNICEF, "At a Glance: Nigeria – Statistics," 2009. www.unicef.org.

in the state, and only 6 of the 15 inspectors had degrees in education and none had specialized training in educational supervision/inspection. This inadequacy may be due to lack of policy on the recruitment and deployment of inspectors. Meanwhile, there is need to have the right quality of inspectors for effective discharge of their duties. [P.M.] Wasanaga (2004) reiterated that inspectors, in order to carry out their duties, should have good academic qualifications, specialized skills and well-established staff development programmes to enable them to keep pace with the changes in the education sector.

In addition to having the right quality and quantity of inspectors, the right tools, enabling environment and effective legal backing is required for the effectiveness of the responsibility of quality assurance agents in the education sector.

Statement of the Problem

The standard of education is continually declining leading to the production of low-quality output who are unable to contribute to societal development. Education stakeholders have blamed the quality assurance agents (inspectors of education) for the falling standard. The complaint is that schools are not regularly inspected and that the quality of inspection is below expectation. According to Ogunu (2001), the number of inspectors is inadequate and a good number of them are said to be unqualified and are not well informed about their responsibilities due to lack of in-service training and workshops. The result of these inadequacies is that the quality of instruction has progressively declined as evidenced by poor performance of students in examination and graduates in their workplaces.

This study therefore is to find out the roles of inspectors of education in Nigeria. Specifically, it seeks the knowledge of inspectors on their basic responsibilities, hindrances to effective performance of their duties and strategies for improvement.

The main purpose of this study therefore is to highlight the problems facing the inspectors of education as quality assurance agents and discuss ways of solving the problems with a view to improve the quality of education in Nigeria.

Discussion of the Result

There seems to have been a realization that the quality of teaching and learning has declined due to ineffective and inefficient inspection of schools. Inspection as a mechanism for accountability is expected to lead to desirable change that would lead to the production of quality outputs in the school system. The statutory functions of the inspectorate service are carried out through regular inspection of schools below the tertiary level, follow-up visits to ensure implementation of recommendations, provision of national guidelines for inspection, accreditation of schools and monitoring learning achievements among others. It is thus obvious that these responsibilities are enormous and require huge amounts of money to meet these needs, especially the provision of serviceable and appropriate vehicles based on the state terrains.

Inadequacy of funds has been a serious constraint to school inspection. [The study] identifies the greatest hindrance to effective inspection as lack of funds while [it] recommends proper funding and purchase of suitable vehicles and other means of transportation based on the local terrain. In order to reinvigorate the inspectorate services, there is need to make adequate financial provisions through budgetary allocations and following due process and effective monitoring to ensure that the monies allocated to the inspectorate are judiciously spent on items they are meant for.

Development and Regular Review
of Inspection Tools

The Nigerian inspection practice has continued to be characterized by traditional visits copied from the United Kingdom model and include advisory visits, full general inspection, recognition inspection, subject inspection, follow-up inspection, etc. Experience has shown that these methods have failed to stop the gradual decline in the quality of education offered in schools. However, inspection practices have been undergoing changes globally even in the UK since the 1980s. The Nigerian inspectorate service is thus faced with the challenges posed by these innovations. The new trends in school inspection include whole school evaluation, school self-evaluation or self-review and systemic evaluation (FME 2006). Monitoring and evaluation are also incorporated in the new type of inspection.

It is obvious that the new approach to school inspection is holistic, involving all aspects of the school system, and if adopted will impact on the effectiveness of inspection in monitoring the quality of learning.

The recent global trends in school inspection call for seminars/workshops where education experts will brainstorm and develop viable and uniform tools for inspection nationwide that would cover all aspects of school life. These may include the inspectors' handbook and uniform instruments for inspection.

These instruments should be constantly reviewed in line with new developments in the school system and the global trends. Secondly, it should move from intuitive judgment to emphasis on school outcomes measured by certain indicators and by observation.

The global concern about school accountability and [its] continued improvement has in turn brought to the fore the crucial responsibilities of the inspectorate service. It is therefore important that after the acquisition of inspection skills, there should be periodic assessment to determine the areas for further training. Wilcox . . . noted that inspection should be the kind of profession that provides the inspector with continuing satisfaction and challenges throughout his career.

Conclusion and Recommendations

Proper and regular inspection has the potential to promote school effectiveness leading to the improvement of the quality of education given to the citizens. From the responses of the federal and state inspectors, the paper revealed that there are many hindrances to effective performance of inspectors' duties. The adherence to traditional inspection practice also has not achieved the desired results of promoting quality education. The paper therefore recommends strategies for improving school inspection. Some of these strategies include provision of adequate funds, development and regular review of inspection tools, employment of qualified and experienced inspectors, induction of new inspectors and capacity building for practicing inspectors and adequate legal provisions for enforcing compliance by schools and proprietors. It noted that if these strategies are well implemented, adequate and effective school inspection will be achieved, leading to the improvement of the quality of education in the country.

> "The proposed law [the Same Sex Marriage (Prohibition) Act] violates Nigeria's commitments under international human rights law."

The Same-Sex Marriage Prohibition Act Is a Violation of Human Rights

Human Rights Watch

Human Rights Watch (HRW) is an international human rights organization. In the following viewpoint, HRW condemns a bill that would imprison for up to five years anyone "who goes through the ceremony of marriage with a person of the same sex" or speaks up or forms a group in support of gay and lesbian rights. Activists charge that it not only infringes on the civil and political freedoms of all Nigerians, but also violates international human rights law.

As you read, consider the following questions:

1. When was the Same Sex Marriage (Prohibition) Act introduced?

2. What international human rights treaty does HRW assert that the bill violates?

3. According to HRW, how many human rights organizations are opposed to the bill and wrote to the Nigerian president to voice their opposition?

A sweepingly homophobic bill being fast-tracked through Nigeria's National Assembly threatens human rights and Nigeria's democratic progress, Human Rights Watch said today [February 18, 2007] in a letter to lawmakers. Human Rights Watch called on legislators to reject the bill, which would imprison anyone who speaks out or forms a group supporting lesbian and gay people's rights, and would silence virtually any public discussion or visibility around lesbian and gay lives.

"This law strikes a blow not just at the rights of lesbian and gay people, but at the civil and political freedoms of all Nigerians," said Scott Long, director of the Lesbian, Gay, Bisexual, and Transgender Rights Program at Human Rights Watch. "But lawmakers are pushing this repressive bill through with a minimum of public scrutiny or debate."

The Same Sex Marriage Act

The bill is entitled the "Same Sex Marriage (Prohibition) Act." In its last published version, it would impose a five-year prison sentence on anyone who "goes through the ceremony of marriage with a person of the same sex." Anyone, including a priest or cleric, who "performs, witnesses, aids or abets the ceremony of same sex marriage," would face the same sentence. It goes beyond that, however, to punish any positive representation of or advocacy for the rights of lesbian and gay people. Anyone "involved in the registration of gay clubs, societies and organizations, sustenance, procession or meetings, publicity and public show of same sex amorous relationship directly or indirectly in public and in private," would be subject to the same sentence.

The legislation was first introduced in January 2006 by Nigeria's minister of justice, Bayo Ojo. It lay dormant for months in the National Assembly, as nationwide elections—scheduled for April 2007—drew near. On February 12, 2007, however, a public hearing was called in the House of Representatives Women's Affairs Committee with only two days' notice. A coalition of Nigerian human rights organizations opposed to the bill was initially told it could not address the hearing, as it was by invitation only. Although the groups were later allowed to speak, the bill has apparently moved forward rapidly in both Nigeria's House and Senate without further public debate. It is reportedly poised for a third reading in the Senate on March 1, after which it could become law.

"If the National Assembly can strip one group of its freedoms, then the liberties of all Nigerians are at risk," said Long. "The secrecy and speed with which this law is being forced forward suggests lawmakers want to hide its threats to Nigeria's democratic progress."

The Role of International Human Rights Law

The proposed law violates Nigeria's commitments under international human rights law. These commitments include the International Covenant on Civil and Political Rights (ICCPR), to which Nigeria acceded without reservations in 1993, and which protects the rights to freedom of expression (article 19), freedom of assembly (article 21) and freedom of association (article 22). The ICCPR affirms the equality of all people before the law and the right to freedom from discrimination in articles 2 and 26. In the landmark 1994 case, *Toonen v. Australia*, the United Nations Human Rights Committee, which monitors states' compliance with the ICCPR, held that sexual orientation should be understood to be a status protected from discrimination under these articles.

Western Anglican Reaction to Same-Sex Marriage Act

For some time, homosexual activity in Nigeria has been legally prohibited, with sanctions of up to 14 years of imprisonment. More recently, legislation was proposed in Nigeria that would ban same-sex blessing or marriage ceremonies, penalize those involved in them, and outlaw efforts to promote same-sex activity of any kind and through any means, with penalties of five years of imprisonment. This proposed legislation has been publicly upheld by the Nigerian Anglican Church, and personally defended by its Primate, Archbishop Peter Akinola. . . . [who] wrote:

> The Church commends the law-makers for their prompt reaction to outlaw same-sex relationships in Nigeria and calls for the bill to be passed since the idea expressed in the bill is the moral position of Nigerians regarding human sexuality.

> Given the highly charged and divisive debate within the Anglican Communion regarding same-sex blessings and the ordination of sexually active homosexuals, the Nigerian legislation and its support by the Anglican Church there has received a good deal of publicity. Many liberal Anglicans have attacked the proposals and the local church's support of them. They have also charged that conservative Anglicans around the world (and especially in America) have failed to confront the seriousness of this situation and, in their eagerness to make common cause with African Anglicans, have actually become complicit in supporting a movement that is grossly abusive of basic human rights.

Ephraim Radner and Andrew Goddard, "Human Rights, Homosexuality and the Anglican Communion: Reflections in Light of Nigeria," Fulcrum, 2006. www.fulcrum-anglican.org.uk.

The African Charter on Human and Peoples' Rights similarly affirms the equality of all people. Its article 2 states: "Every individual shall be entitled to the enjoyment of the rights and freedoms recognized and guaranteed in the present Charter without distinction of any kind such as race, ethnic group, color, sex, language, religion, political or any other opinion, national and social origin, fortune, birth or other status." Article 3 guarantees every individual equality before the law. And its article 26 prescribes that: "Every individual shall have the duty to respect and consider his fellow beings without discrimination, and to maintain relations aimed at promoting, safeguarding and reinforcing mutual respect and tolerance."

Reaction of the United States

The US State Department released a statement in February 2006 condemning the proposed legislation. It stated it was "concerned by reports of legislation in Nigeria that would restrict or prohibit citizens from assembling, organizing, holding events or rallies, and participating in ceremonies of religious union, based upon sexual orientation and gender identity. . . . The freedoms of speech, association, expression, assembly, and religion are long-standing international commitments and are universally recognized. Nigeria, as a State Party to the International Covenant on Civil and Political Rights, has assumed important obligations on these matters. We expect the Government of Nigeria to act in a manner consistent with those obligations."

In a March 2006 letter to President Olusegun Obasanjo, a coalition of 16 human rights organizations—in Nigeria, elsewhere in Africa, and internationally—urged him to disavow the bill.

On February 23, 2007, four United Nations independent experts on human rights also condemned the bill. They stated, "In addition to clear elements of discrimination and persecution on the basis of sexual orientation, the Bill contains provisions that infringe freedoms of assembly and association and imply serious consequences for the exercise of the freedom of expression and opinion." They added that it would "have a chilling effect for local human rights defenders who undertake peaceful advocacy on the adverse human rights implications of the law for lesbian, gay, bisexual and transgender persons."

| "The so-called 'right' to homosexual orientation threatens the order of society because the continuation of the race is threatened by gay practice."

The Same-Sex Marriage Prohibition Act Strengthens Traditional Marriage

Anglican Communion

The Anglican Communion is an international association of national and regional Anglican churches. In the following viewpoint, the organization reiterates its support for the act that prohibits same-sex marriage in Nigeria, contending that the bill reinforces the institution of traditional marriage and prevents the influence of a damaging and permissive Western culture. The organization cites support for their view from the Bible as well as Nigerian social convention, both of which consider homosexuality a threat to Nigerian society.

As you read, consider the following questions:

1. What texts from the Old Testament does the Anglican Communion cite in their argument against same-sex marriage?

2. According to the Anglican Communion, are there any mentions of the marriage bond between same-sex partners in the Bible?

3. What church has the primate, or senior bishop, called to be disciplined for its support for same-sex unions?

The Church of Nigeria (Anglican Communion) is a Bible-based and spiritually dynamic Church that seeks to epitomise the genuine love of Christ. The Church's attitude to homosexuality is rooted in biblical values and pre-supposed by a high view of Scripture.

The Primate of all Nigeria has said, "Our argument is that, if homosexuals see themselves as deviants who have gone astray, the Christian spirit would plead for patience and prayers to make room for their repentance. When scripture says something is wrong and some people say that it is right, such people make God a liar. We argue that it is a blatant lie against Almighty God that homosexuality is their God-given urge and inclination. For us, it is better seen as an acquired aberration."

The Church of Nigeria sees its view as based upon the witness of Scripture. The House of Bishops issued a detailed and clearly argued statement. In it there are discussed four texts from the Old Testament which speak specifically of homosexual acts. These are Genesis 19:5, Leviticus 18:22, Leviticus 18:27 and Judges 19:22. All these texts show how homosexuality is regarded as an abominable deed. The statement concludes: "Thus it is clear from the passages considered that the Old Testament regards homosexuality as an atrocious and unnatural act. The Mosaic Law is against it and stipulates capital punishment for the offender. It is classified among the most offensive crimes like idolatry involving the sacrifice of children, having intercourse with animals, or marrying a woman and her mother."

Conclusions of the Church of Nigeria

The report continues by considering the New Testament. From Romans 1:26–27, 1 Corinthians 6:9,10, and 1 Timothy 1:9,10 and concludes:

- First, we find a strong denunciation of homosexual acts as being contrary to nature and against God's revealed will for mankind.

- Next, homosexuality is found in the catalogue of practices regarded as unrighteous and therefore a disqualification for inheritance of the kingdom of God. Although the practice was known in the Semitic world and acknowledged as widespread in the Hellenistic world, it is portrayed as a classical indication of the final stage of perversion or depravity on which divine wrath rests, with little or no hope of repentance.

- Thirdly, although homosexuality is not singled out as the only grievous sin that attracts God's judgment, whether in the Old or New Testament, homosexual acts are seen appropriately as pagan acts unworthy of a person who has a true knowledge of God, and both fears and worships Him.

- Finally, neither in the Old Testament nor in the New do we have any record, or even mention, trace or hint concerning marriage bond between same-sex partners. There were cases of attempted acts of homosexuality and reference to homosexual customs, seen as aberrations and perversions. Though such acts or customs were known among nations outside Israel and were reported as common among former inhabitants of the land of Canaan, there is no hint that those engaged in the acts ever finally settled down to a lasting union with their same-sex partners.

In Nigerian traditional culture homosexuality is seen as taboo. Homosexuals are thought of as threatening the divinely ordained order of the community. The Western idea of human rights is subservient to the service of the common good. The so-called 'right' to homosexual orientation threatens the order of society because the continuation of the race is threatened by gay practice. Children are treasured as fruits of marriage and any union, as a gay union, that prevents the propagation of the community's growth is a personal shame to be openly censured.

The Church of Nigeria (Anglican Communion) has therefore strongly opposed the developments in the Episcopal Church (USA), the Church of Canada and the Church of England. The Primate [senior bishop] has called for the Church of England to be disciplined within the Anglican Communion for its response to the Civil Partnership Act.

Strengthening Traditional Marriage

In Nigeria the Same Sex Marriage (Prohibition) Act 2006 is passing through the legislature. The House of Bishops has supported it because we understand that it is designed to strengthen traditional marriage and family life and to prevent wholesale importation of currently damaging Western values. It bans same-sex unions, all homosexual acts and the formation of any gay groups. The Standing Committee of the Church of Nigeria has twice commended the act in their Message to the Nation.

A statement of the House of Bishops makes it clear that the Church of Nigeria is committed to the pastoral care of homosexual people. It says: "While recognising the sinfulness, from the biblical perspective, of homosexuality, we must continue to keep open the door of restoration for homosexuals through repentance on the one hand, and sensitive pastoral care, on the other." The Church is clear that all people are sinners and need to repent. What it will not do is bless sinful lifestyles.

Periodical and Internet Sources Bibliography

The following articles have been selected to supplement the diverse views presented in this chapter.

Accelerator

"Government's Non-Challancy Towards Public Schools," January 7, 2009.

Shyamantha Asokan

"Nigeria's Gay Church Is Reborn amid a Climate of Fear," *Guardian* (UK), April 24, 2011.

Sade Ayodele

"Incessant Runway Incursions Expose the Dangers at Nigerian Airports," *Business Day*, March 17, 2011.

Mark Gongloff

"Nigeria's Power Problem," *Environmental Capital* (blog), October 30, 2007. http://blogs.wsj.com.

Guardian (Nigeria)

"The Bauchi Airstrip and Aviation Breaches," March 14, 2011.

Savitri Hensman

"Nigeria's Attack on Human Rights Has No Virtue," *Guardian* (UK), March 19, 2009.

Timothy Jumbo

"Power Sector Privatisation: Indians Again?," *Vanguard*, March 21, 2011.

Owei Lakemfa

"Walking Education on Its Head," *Vanguard*, March 23, 2011.

Ibraheem Musa

"Women's Rights Are Still Being Abused," *Daily Trust*, December 11, 2009.

Helen Ovbiagele

"Power Supply: A Permanent Problem?," *Vanguard*, February 13 2011.

Quadry Wasiu

"Solution to Nigeria Power Outrage," Booksie, May 9, 2008. www.booksie.com.

For Further Discussion

Chapter 1

1. There was much concern over the 2011 presidential elections. John Campbell worried that the elections might push the country to the brink of disaster. *THISDAY* argued that Nigeria would rise to the occasion. Do you think Campbell's worries were well founded? How do you think Nigeria avoided much of the violence and unrest that the country had endured in earlier election cycles?

2. Adewale T. Akande argued that the 2011 presidential elections presented a chance for Nigerians to rid their country of corrupt officials. Dafe Onojovwo maintained that the elections would do little to bring about any significant reform in Nigeria. Which author do you think made the most persuasive argument and why? Offer examples from the viewpoints to support your answer.

Chapter 2

1. Louise Arbour promotes Nigeria's intervention in the Ivory Coast conflict. Alex Engwete argues that Nigeria should not take a larger role in the Ivory Coast crisis. Read both viewpoints. Which argument is the most persuasive and why?

2. The Plateau region of Nigeria has been afflicted with chronic violence. Joseph Bottum classifies it as a sectarian problem. Peter Cunliffe-Jones argues that the violence is rooted in economic inequality. What is your opinion? Use the viewpoints to inform your view.

3. Should national unity be a top priority in Nigeria? Sam Adesua believes national integration can be achieved. Osita Ebiem contends that Nigeria will never be fully uni-

fied and should be divided along sectarian lines. After reading both opinions, which do you feel holds the best hope for the Nigerian people?

4. The Niger Delta is a troubled and complicated region. Read viewpoints written by Kelly Campbell, Judith Burdin Asuni, and Ebrima Sillah and Sam Olukoya. Which option is the most promising? Which one do you feel would be the least effective in addressing the violence in the region?

Chapter 3

1. How bad is the problem of corruption in Nigeria? Read viewpoints written by Lanre Akinola and Jideofor Adibe to inform your answer.

2. Terence P. McCulley emphasizes the importance of fair and transparent elections to bring about change in Nigeria. Olumide Taiwo and Nelipher Moyo argue that improving transparency and accountability can rid Nigeria of corruption. Do you think that if Nigerians demand more accountability and transparency from their officials that real change can occur in their country? Why or why not?

Chapter 4

1. After reading the viewpoints in this chapter, which challenge of the ones presented do you think is the most important for Nigeria's future? Why?

2. Human Rights Watch has criticized Nigeria's treatment of gays, particularly its proposed prohibition of same-sex marriage. The Anglican Communion argues the ban is necessary to protect Nigeria against destructive Western values. Do you think same-sex marriage is an option for Nigeria? How should Nigeria treat same-sex couples?

Organizations to Contact

The editors have compiled the following list of organizations concerned with the issues debated in this book. The descriptions are derived from materials provided by the organizations. All have publications or information available for interested readers. The list was compiled on the date of publication of the present volume; names, addresses, phone and fax numbers, and e-mail and Internet addresses may change. Be aware that many organizations take several weeks or longer to respond to inquiries, so allow as much time as possible.

Amnesty International (AI)
5 Penn Plaza, 16th Floor, New York, NY 10001
(212) 807-8400 • fax: (212) 627-1451
e-mail: admin-us@aiusa.org
website: www.amnesty.org

Established in 1961, Amnesty International (AI) is one of the premier independent human rights organizations in the world. AI is made up of 2.8 million members, supporters, and activists who work together to address human rights abuses in more than 150 countries and territories. AI members and activists mobilize letter-writing campaigns, mass demonstrations, vigils, and direct lobbying efforts on behalf of individuals and groups being oppressed, tortured, and imprisoned for political, economic, social, or cultural reasons. Every year AI publishes the influential *State of the World's Human Rights* report, which assesses the global state of human rights. It also publishes monthly e-newsletters, *Stop Violence Against Women* and *Counter Terror with Justice.*

Economic and Financial Crimes Commission (EFCC)
No. 5 Fomella Street, Off Adetokunbo Ademola Crescent
Wuse II, Abuja
  Nigeria

+234 9-6717419 • fax: +234 9-6715371
website: www.efccnigeria.org

The Economic and Financial Crimes Commission (EFCC) is the Nigerian agency tasked with eliminating corruption by investigating and prosecuting financial crimes; identifying and confiscating illegally acquired wealth; protecting foreign and domestic investment in the country and its businesses from graft and fraud; and launching a campaign to challenge public and governmental tolerance of corruption. The goal is to change long-held attitudes about the scourge of corruption in order to improve Nigeria's government services and business environment and change the country's reputation as tolerant of corruption in the private and public arenas. The EFCC website offers information on high-profile cases and prosecutions, the latest news on ongoing initiatives, and press releases from the EFCC offices. The EFCC also publishes a periodical, the *Milestone*, which chronicles efforts to fight corruption in Nigeria.

Empretec Nigeria Foundation

Plot 15E, Flat 2, Muri Okunola Street, PO Box 71003
Victoria Island, Lagos
Nigeria
+234-1-898 2231
e-mail: admin@empretecnigeriafoundation.org
website: www.empretecnigeriafoundation.org

Empretec Nigeria Foundation is a nongovernmental organization (NGO) that promotes small and medium business enterprises and efforts to make Nigeria more globally competitive. The organization develops and supports initiatives to increase productivity and efficiency in the private and public sector. One of Empretec's key areas is training for business leaders at workshops and conferences. The organization also offers networking opportunities for entrepreneurs, financiers, and other business figures. Empretec Nigeria is part of a larger NGO, Empretec Africa.

Energy Commission of Nigeria (ECN)

Plot 701C, Central Business District, P.M.B. 358, Garki, Abuja
    Nigeria
+234 09-5234920 • fax: +234 09-5234922
e-mail: officialmail@energy.gov.ng
website: www.energy.gov.ng

The Energy Commission of Nigeria (ECN) is the governmental agency responsible for coordinating and supervising the country's energy activities, including developing and implementing energy initiatives. Other goals include guaranteeing a stable and sustainable energy supply for Nigeria's growing business sector as well as existing homes, institutions, and businesses; promoting efficient use of energy resources; and facilitating indigenous participation in the energy sector. The ECN website details current programs and projects, features a photo archive, and posts breaking news and press releases. It also offers a document library, which includes bulletins, reports, brochures, transcripts of meetings and seminars, and topic briefs.

Federal Airports Authority of Nigeria (FAAN)

Murtala Muhammed Airport, Ikeja, Lagos
    Nigeria
+234 01-4970335 • fax: +234 01-4970342
e-mail: contact@faannigeria.org
website: www.faannigeria.org

The Federal Airports Authority of Nigeria (FAAN) is in charge of managing and protecting the nation's airports. FAAN's mission is to "develop and profitably manage customer centric airport facilities for safe, secure, and efficient carriage of passengers and goods at world class standards." With the issue of safety and security in the news, FAAN is working to implement better policies to protect airport facilities and fight terrorism. The FAAN website features updates on those efforts as well as other programs and initiatives to make Nigeria's airports more efficient, attractive, and user friendly. The website also hosts a discussion forum to exchange news and ideas on Nigeria's airports and airlines.

Human Rights Watch (HRW)

350 Fifth Avenue, 34th Floor, New York, NY 10118
(212) 290-4700 • fax: (212) 736-1300
e-mail: hrwpress@hrw.org
website: www.hrw.org

Founded in 1978, Human Rights Watch (HRW) is a non-profit, independent human rights group that researches and publishes more than one hundred reports in order to shed light on pressing human rights abuses. Often working in difficult situations—including oppressive and tyrannical governments—HRW strives to provide accurate and impartial reporting on human rights conditions for the media, financial institutions, and international organizations. The group's wide-ranging and thorough reports can be accessed on the HRW website. Interested viewers can also access video, audio, podcasts, photo essays, and photo galleries.

International Gay & Lesbian Human Rights Commission (IGLHRC)

80 Maiden Lane, Suite 1505, New York, NY 10038
(212) 430-6054 • fax: (212) 430-6060
e-mail: iglhrc@iglhrc.org
website: www.iglhrc.org

The International Gay & Lesbian Human Rights Commission (IGLHRC) is an independent international organization working to advance the human rights protection of gay and lesbians and others discriminated against because of their actual or perceived sexual orientation, gender identity, or expression. To this end, the IGLHRC builds advocacy partnerships with local activists to address pressing human rights issues and strengthen local human rights frameworks. It also works to connect local and regional activists with international organizations such as the United Nations and nongovernmental organizations. The IGLHRC publishes a series of reports on the state of human rights in a number of countries, annual reports, the *Outspoken* newsletter, and training materials.

National Agency for the Control of AIDS (NACA)

Plot 823 Ralph Sodeinde Street, CBD, Abuja
  Nigeria
+234 9-461-3724 • fax: +234 9-461-3700
e-mail: info@naca.gov.ng
website: www.naca.gov.ng

The National Agency for the Control of AIDS (NACA) is the Nigerian governmental agency tasked with developing and supervising AIDS policies, coordinating efforts of governmental and nongovernmental organizations, and monitoring the progression of the epidemic in the nation. The agency trains health professionals and community health leaders in AIDS policy and treatment advances, establishes resource centers in local communities, and disseminates information for communities and individuals on the disease. The NACA website offers access to a range of reports, press releases, statistical information, and policy briefs.

National Broadcasting Commission (NBC)

Plot 20, Ibrahim Taiwo Street, Asokoro, Abuja
  Nigeria
+234 9-7805730
e-mail: info@nbc.gov.ng
website: www.nbc.gov.ng

The National Broadcasting Commission (NBC) is a Nigerian governmental agency responsible for promoting and monitoring a sustainable and robust broadcasting sector in the country. It develops broadcasting standards and formulates regulations and guidelines; issues licenses for terrestrial TV and radio services, cable television, satellite radio, and DTH providers; and works to improve access to and the quality of the Nigerian broadcasting sector. NBC publishes an e-newsletter that can be accessed through the agency's website. It offers information on recent initiatives and issues under consideration or debate at the NBC. The website also features a forum and welcomes feedback from concerned citizens and stakeholders.

Niger Delta Development Commission (NDDC)

31 Haile Selaissie, Asokoro, Abuja
  Nigeria
e-mail: info@nddc.gov.ng
website: www.nddc.gov.ng

Founded in 2000, the Niger Delta Development Commission (NDDC) was created to facilitate the sustainable and effective development of the Niger Delta region in Nigeria. The NDDC formulates policy and guidelines for development; plans, monitors, and implements construction of infrastructure, businesses, housing, and government services; works to encourage sustainable development while protecting human rights and the environment; and makes sure businesses, especially oil and gas companies, follow all national and regional laws and regulations. The latest news and information on NDDC programs, policies, and activities can be found on the agency's website.

Bibliography of Books

Ignatius Adeh   *Corruption and Environmental Law: The Case of the Niger Delta*. London: Global, 2010.

Said Adejumobi, ed.   *Governance and Politics in Post-Military Nigeria: Changes and Challenges*. New York: Palgrave Macmillan, 2010.

Said Adejumobi, ed.   *State, Economy, and Society in Post-Military Nigeria*. New York: Palgrave Macmillan, 2011.

John Campbell   *Nigeria: Dancing on the Brink*. Lanham, MD: Rowman & Littlefield, 2011.

Pádraig Risteard Carmody   *The New Scramble for Africa*. Malden, MA: Polity Press, 2011.

Dike-Ogu Chukwumerije   *One Nigeria: The Birth and Evolution of an Idea*. London: Afriscope, 2011.

Peter Cunliffe-Jones   *My Nigeria: Five Decades of Independence*. New York: Palgrave Macmillan, 2010.

David T. Doris   *Vigilant Things: On Thieves, Yoruba Anti-Aesthetics, and the Strange Fates of Ordinary Objects in Nigeria*. Seattle: University of Washington Press, 2011.

E.C. Ejiogu   *The Roots of Political Instability in Nigeria*. Burlington, VT: Ashgate Publishing, 2011.

Toyin Falola and *Nigeria, Nationalism, and Writing*
Saheed Aderinto *History*. Rochester, NY: University of
Rochester Press, 2010.

Iyorwuese H. *Nigeria: After the Nightmare.*
Hagher Lanham, MD: University Press of
America, 2011.

John Iliffe *Obasanjo, Nigeria and the World.*
Rochester, NY: James Currey, 2011.

Attahiru M. Jega *Nigeria at Fifty: Contributions to*
and Jacqueline W. *Peace, Democracy, and Development.*
Farris Abuja, Nigeria: Shehu Musa Yar'Adua
Foundation, 2010.

Ebenezer Obadare *Nigeria at Fifty: The Nation in*
and Wale *Narration.* Abingdon, United
Adebanwi, eds. Kingdom: Routledge, 2010.

Cyril Obi and Siri *Oil and Insurgency in the Niger Delta:*
Aas Rustad *Managing the Complex Politics of*
Petro-Violence. New York: Zed Books,
2011.

Victor Ojakorotu *Anatomy of the Niger Delta Crisis:*
Causes, Consequences, and
Opportunities for Peace. London:
Global, 2010.

Okechukwu Oko *Key Problems for Democracy in*
Nigeria: Credible Elections,
Corruption, Security, Governance, and
Political Parties. Lewiston, NY: Edwin
Mellen Press, 2010.

Adebayo Olukoshi *Beyond the State: Nigeria's Search for*
Positive Leadership. Ibadan, Nigeria:
Ibadan University Press, 2005.

Michael Peel   *A Swamp Full of Dollars: Pipelines and Paramilitaries at Nigeria's Oil Frontier.* Chicago, IL: Lawrence Hill Books, 2010.

Max Siollun   *Oil, Politics, and Violence: Nigeria's Coup Culture.* New York: Algora Publishers, 2009.

Chris Stokel-Walker   *African Lions: The Colonial Geopolitics of Africa's Gas & Oil.* Raleigh, NC: Lulu, 2011.

G.N. Uzoigwe   *Visions of Nationhood: Prelude to the Nigerian Civil War.* Trenton, NJ: Africa World Press, 2011.

Index

ML   3/12